JIM RYUN
Master of the Mile

Jim Ryun has been acknowledged by track experts as the greatest middle-distance runner in history. John Lake tells of the painful self-discipline, fears, disappointments and triumphs that are all part of Ryun's amazing career.

JIM RYUN
Master of the Mile

by John Lake

Illustrated with Photographs

Random House
New York

Library of Congress Catalog Card Number: 68-14488
Manufactured in the United States of America
Text design by Jackie Mabli
Cover design by Ted Burwell

Photograph credits: A.F. P. from Pictorial, 95; Phil Bath for *Sports Illustrated,* © Time Inc., 53; Rich Clarkson, cover, front and back endpapers, i, ii, vi, 2, 4, 9, 11, 12, 16, 28, 34, 42, 46, 49, 56, 59, 67, 69, 99, 101, 105, 107, 112, 113, 117, 129, 130, 132, 133, 135, 137, 141, 143, 145, 147, 158, 162, 164, 169, 171; *Paris Match,* 87; Ken Regan, 152-153; UPI, 88, 122; Wide World, 6, 125, 143.

CONTENTS

Foreword

My fastest time for the mile was 4 minutes and 51 seconds. That was 20 years ago on a sweltering afternoon in Saratoga Springs, New York. After I had completed the distance, I thought my arms and legs were going to fall off. It was a milestone in my life, though. I passed another milestone—on the road to old-fogeyism—in July, 1966, on the day Jim Ryun set a world record at Berkeley, California, by running the mile in 3:51.3. I should have been delighted, because at the moment Jim hit the tape, more than two million copies of my *Newsweek* magazine cover story dealing with his achievements were rolling off the presses in Dayton, Ohio. Instead, my reaction was horror. A "little kid" had run the mile almost a full minute faster than I had.

viii

Of course, as most followers of track know, Jim Ryun is no ordinary "little kid." And the reason for this distinction is his indomitable will coupled with an extraordinary ability.

As I write this, Jim is on the threshold of manhood, and I am confident that he will be a fine man who will lead a responsible, rewarding life. I am grateful to him for the example he has set for my own son, Eric, and for other boys, of all ages. He has taught all of us some important things about self-discipline and will power.

I am thankful to Jim and to his coaches, Bob Timmons and J. D. Edmiston, for the time they spent with me and the help they gave. I am thankful, too, for the cooperation and friendship of Mr. and Mrs. Gerald Ryun of Wichita, Bob Kyle of Wichita, Rich Clarkson of Topeka and Jim Benagh of New York. This book could not have been written without them. Nor could it have been published without the assistance of my editor, Zander Hollander, and my typist, Mary Hood.

I affectionately dedicate my efforts to that perfectly marvelous girl who made me want to write a book in the first place.

JOHN E. LAKE

Teaneck, New Jersey
May, 1967

JIM RYUN
Master of the Mile

1

The Marvelous Mile

"Last call for the mile run."

This was the announcement the crowd of 15,000 was waiting for. Grandstand noises dwindled to a murmur as six runners nervously approached the starting line. They fumbled with their sweat suits. They flexed their legs. They bounced lightly on the cinder composition track.

The weather in Berkeley, California, that afternoon of July 17, 1966, was ideal for running—76 degrees and sunny. Up on the rim of Edwards Stadium, blue and gold pennants fluttered lightly. Loudspeakers blared. ". . . And in lane number two, the amazing freshman from the University of Kansas . . ."

Jim Ryun heard his own name echoing in the infield. The slender youngster straightened up, jabbed

The runners leave their marks as the starter's gun signals the beginning of the race.

his spikes into the hard-packed track and jogged several quick steps. He barely noticed the cheering and applauding. Spectators were concentrating on Ryun. Ryun was concentrating on the race.

Then the runners were ordered to their marks. The starter's voice sounded sharply over the buzzing of the crowd. "Get set . . ." And suddenly the pistol cracked, blasting away the tension.

Now that the race was on, Jim Ryun sensed nothing except the shoving and scurrying of the crowded rush to the first turn. Spiked shoes thudded on the track. Ryun snorted, gulped air and settled swiftly into his stride. His breath flowed easily. His legs pumped hard. The crowd might scream itself hoarse, but Ryun wouldn't hear. Until the race was over, no sound would reach his ears except the announcements of the runners' times.

As the first call was given loudly and clearly, Ryun felt relief. "Twenty-nine . . . one." The time for the first half-lap was 29.1 seconds, a fine pace, he thought. In some races it was hard to know if you were running fast enough. Sometimes, too, the timers didn't seem to care. But today everything seemed to go perfectly.

The bunched-up runners sped past the 220-yard mark. Tom Von Ruden of Oklahoma State led the pack by several strides. Richard Romo of Texas was next. Ryun was in third place, his stride relaxed and easy. The tall, skinny Kansas kid seemed to be everybody's favorite—including the timers'. He was the runner the timers shouted at, straining to make their voices clear, because just as much as the fans, they also wanted to see a world record. Ryun was the racer who could set it for them.

Only six weeks earlier, the 19-year-old University of Kansas freshman had clipped off a stunningly fast mile in 3 minutes, 53.7 seconds. He had missed tying the world mark by the narrowest of margins—one-tenth of a second. Now, on this bright, warm Sunday afternoon, the crowd was rooting for him to shatter Frenchman Michel Jazy's world mark of 3:53.6.

Still running smoothly on the heels of the laboring Von Ruden, Ryun heard the call for the next half lap, telling him that he had completed a quarter-mile in 57.7 seconds. Before the racers swung single file into the next turn, public-address speakers boomed Ryun's time. Excited fans shouted encouragement.

Suddenly there was something new to shout about. Dark-haired, thick-chested Richard Romo charged past both Ryun and Von Ruden. The race had a new leader. Abruptly, Von Ruden fell back. Ryun kept up his steady clip, just a few feet behind the new pacesetter.

To Ryun it seemed obvious that a distinct pattern was taking shape during the course of the race. First one opponent, then another had spurted recklessly into the lead. Obviously, neither could hope to maintain the fast early pace. It occurred to Ryun,

Ryun runs easily behind the new pacesetter, Richard Romo (3).

and to many spectators, too, that the other runners were burning themselves out in an attempt to provide a record early speed in order to pull Ryun along until he was ready to launch his own finishing kick. Excitement mounted in the grandstand. A record mile? It seemed possible.

Ryun's legs were beginning to feel heavy. His sore left knee, swabbed with ointment before the race, burned hotly. He still had too far to run, too much to think about to let his mind focus on Jazy's magic 3:53.6 figure.

Pounding into the home stretch for the second time, he again heard the sound of accelerating footsteps behind him. He wondered if it could be another pacesetter. It was indeed. This time Wade Bell of Oregon sped eagerly to the head of the pack as the field flashed past the starting line again. Speakers quickly broadcast Ryun's time for the half-mile: 1 minute, 55.4 seconds.

Spectators chattered. Surely Bell couldn't last. But could Ryun? He was running strongly, wasn't he? Was there a real chance for a world record? Could the fleet college freshman run another half-mile in less than two minutes? How much less?

The stands rocked with cheers as Ryun swung wide on the backstretch and galloped ahead to take the lead for the first time. But a San Francisco sports writer in the press box groaned as he saw Bell struggle bravely to stay ahead, then fall back behind Ryun. "Ryun will never get it now," muttered the reporter.

Like other experts in the crowd—the coaches, the other runners, the knowledgeable track fans—he realized the enormity of Ryun's task. With more than three-eighths of a mile remaining, the star miler had already withered his competition. Nobody was left to push him to the record everyone wanted to see.

Weary Wade Bell had expended so much energy that he wondered if he had saved enough to finish the race. He could hardly believe Ryun's speed and stamina as the youth sped away from him. Later Bell admitted, "Romo and Von Ruden were talking before the race, so I guess they planned to set a fast pace for Ryun on purpose. But that isn't what I was trying to do. I knew I didn't have much chance, but I wanted to win the race. I knew the only way I could do that was to stay with Ryun. Otherwise I could never catch anybody with his speed at the finish."

The finish, however, wasn't on Ryun's mind yet. He was still worried about the third lap. Almost unconsciously, most milers tend to let up on their next-to-last lap. Now, especially with no opponent to spur him on, Ryun needed will power. All alone now, the resolute teen-ager swept past the stands. The gun barked, signaling one lap to go. Even before the loud-speakers bellowed, "Two minutes, 55 seconds," every spectator in the University of California stadium was standing. Nobody could help Jim Ryun now, not even the thousands of screaming fans who realized a record *was* possible. They sensed the ordeal of the skinny, hollow-cheeked boy in his pursuit of an un-

Ryun crosses the finish line as officials record his time with their stopwatches.

yielding enemy—the clock. Ryun's lungs ached. His muscles strained. His throat burned.

Cheering swelled in the stands as the lad in the pale red shorts and blue jersey swept around the last turn and sprinted for the thin white string stretched across the track. Knees and elbows, knees and elbows, Ryun drove for the finish line, fighting for the last few precious tenths of a second. Then he threw back his shoulders and surged across, snapping the taut twine with his body.

A pack of photographers, backpedaling furiously, surrounded the exhausted Ryun and swirled around him as he slowed to a jog and veered off the running surface onto the grass. He was depressed because he felt that he hadn't run fast enough in the last quarter.

Almost at once, indistinct shouts reached him from across the infield, but he could not make out what was being said. He was hopeful but not certain that his time was sufficient for a record. Then he heard the announcement on the loud speakers. Three stop-watches had timed him identically. Ryun's eyes widened. He grinned, shaking his head in amazement and delight. There was no question about it: a record, and what a record! Jim Ryun, 19 years old, had run the mile in 3 minutes, 51.3 seconds, riddling the world mark by nearly two-and-a-half seconds.

It was impossible to quiet the crowd after the official announcement was made. Ryun slowly circled the track several times, gulping air and soothing his strained muscles. One after another, his fellow milers

Barefooted, Ryun jogs his official victory lap.

pumped his hand. Von Ruden, Romo and Bell had been so spent by their early efforts that they had finished far back. Veteran miler Cary Weisiger had finished second, a full 50 yards behind Ryun.

"The other guys were real great," Ryun gratefully told a cluster of demanding reporters. "Wade saved the day. He picked up the pace just at the point it was beginning to lag a little."

Lag a little? Wade Bell chuckled. How nice it would be to lag at that speed in all his races. A few

Accompanied by youthful track fans, Ryun sprints across the Berkeley campus.

minutes later, Bell joined in the applause as the barefooted Ryun pranced onto the track for his official victory lap. He jogged it slowly and modestly, white spiked shoes in his hand and eyes cast downward at the cinder path.

As he left the stadium, clawing souvenir hunters tried to tear off his uniform. It was a moment to enjoy, but enjoying it was impossible. In desperation, Ryun realized that, unless he raced for cover, he would leave Edwards Stadium wearing nothing but his birthday suit. Helpfully, Kansas teammate John Lawson offered to bring along Ryun's track satchel. Bounding across the lawns of the Berkeley campus,

Ryun made his final sprint of the historic afternoon, only to find the lobby of his dormitory jammed with eager well-wishers. Laughing, he dashed up to his room, taking the steps two at a time.

Jim Ryun was a very famous boy. The news rocketed around the globe. Thirty-two years earlier, Kansan Glenn Cunningham had set the world record for the mile. Now, after all that time, the record had come back to the United States. An editorial in *The New York Times* praised the amazing achievement of an athlete so young, and added:

> A track man's real challenge is to himself. It is the frailty of his own muscles, lungs and heart that he must overcome . . . A few poems last forever, but no track records. Yet few endeavors reduce to a purity of concept the nature of all human achievement, as this one does . . . Ryun's record will not last. One can reasonably hope that it will be broken, again and again, by the likable University of Kansas freshman himself. He is just finding his stride.

This last statement pointed out the most significant aspect of Ryun's career. His world-record mile, coming less than three months after his 19th birthday, was his tenth sub-four-minute mile. And in the nine weeks preceding his smashing performance in the All-American Invitation at Berkeley, Ryun had set a United States record by running the two-mile in 8:25.2 at the Coliseum Relays in Los Angeles. He had also broken the world record by running the half-mile in 1:44.9 at the National Track and Field Federation meet in Terre Haute, Indiana.

Suddenly the slim Kansas youth owned almost every important middle-distance mark worth owning. As experts pointed out, even the record for the 1,500-meters was well within Ryun's reach at Berkeley. Timers clocked him in 3:36.1 at the 1,500-meter mark, but, because he still had 118 yards more to run in the slightly longer mile event, Ryun wasn't sprinting his fastest. Even so, he missed Australian Herb Elliott's record for the Olympic-distance "metric mile" by just a half-second.

Ryun was hounded for interviews. For days, wherever he went, the phone jangled continually. "Jim Ryun? He can't talk now. He's in the shower," explained a beefy shot-putter to one caller. "What? I told you he was in the shower 45 minutes ago? Well, Jim Ryun is a very clean boy."

Radio and television newscasts flashed the word of a new world sports hero. It was thrilling news in Los Angeles and New York, in London and Paris, in Sydney and Stockholm and Moscow—and in all the other places where youngsters raced one another over fields and parks and paved streets. Jim Ryun was the envy of all boys who had ever imagined themselves in a real race for fame and glory. In fact, Jim Ryun himself had run mock races with his playmates and dreamed the same boyhood dreams just a few short years before.

2

Some Kids
Just Don't Have It

Even for a weak, skinny boy who had allergies, it was fun growing up in Wichita, Kansas, in the 1950s. Frivolity was forbidden, but to little Jim Ryun (his parents always called him James) it seemed that fun could be found almost anywhere. There were ball games, toy sailboats and a procession of pets in the little house on South Edgemoor Street.

It seemed, though, that his mother was always reminding him, "James, it's time for your medicine." There was visit after visit to Dr. Moseley, the family doctor. When Jim was only 18 months old he had suffered from a hernia. Later, he developed another hernia, which bothered him until he was 12 years old, when it was repaired by surgery. He was also allergic to dust, feathers and pollen and, as a result, he was given an anti-allergy injection once every week.

It certainly was true that many boys and girls had more time for play than the Ryun children. Every Wednesday night and twice on Sundays, Gerald Ryun packed his boys, Jerry and James, into the car, along with their mother and little sister Jeanette, for the familiar trip to the Elpyco Church of Christ. Gerald Ryun's children were brought up on the teachings of the Bible. Religion was the center of their home life. Dancing was frowned on, but the church fellowship provided many games and glad times: roller skating once a month at Skateland, and bowling at the Rose Bowl every Saturday. There was even church league basketball. The two boys were fond of toy sailboats. And for more than five years, the children had a loveable pet cocker spaniel named Bubbles. Jim was Bubbles' favorite.

Jim's parents, his brother, Jerry, and sister, Jeanette, at their home on South Edgemoor Street. Jeanette is tasting Jim's birthday cake.

As soon as he was old enough, Jim joined the Little League. But his progress was discouraging. He often wondered when he would grow big and strong enough to fire the ball from third base to first base without a bounce. But then, he wasn't going to be a big league ballplayer anyhow. After all, sports and games were only spare-time fun. Real-life athletes belonged to another world—even the high school boys who ran and jumped and pole-vaulted on the huge campus at Southeast High, less than a block from the Ryuns' house. It was a world young James Ryun never dreamed of entering. Even when he played on a championship baseball team in the Wichita Sheriff's League, he felt like a pretender. He envied the home-run hitters and the fast-ball pitchers.

"I wish I could play sports well," he thought wistfully. "But some kids have the talent to do those things and other kids don't. I don't have it, that's all."

At Curtis Junior High, Ryun was finally introduced to track. But it embarrassed him even more than most sports. He never seemed to succeed. As a seventh-grader, he tried the hurdles. As an eighth-grader, he tried the 100-yard dash. Jim enjoyed running after school with the other boys. He liked the companionship. But try as he might, he never qualified for a meet. Several times he tried too hard and had to miss practice to rest his strained muscles.

He finally decided that if he wanted to run he would have to try an event that the other boys didn't like. So in ninth grade he tried the longest race open to junior-high boys—the quarter-mile. Still he wasn't good enough. In time trials before the Curtis team's last spring meet, he almost caught the third-place finisher with a burst of energy in the last 200 yards. It was tantalizingly close. James came within a few feet of making the team. Stubbornly he determined to keep trying.

Often in the summer of 1962, skinny, 15-year-old James Ryun would gallop down South Edgemoor Street as far as busy Kellogg Avenue, then come puffing back, dripping with sweat. He felt foolish sometimes. But he wanted to make a high-school team—any team—and it might as well be the track team. After all, he wasn't very good at anything else.

East High in Wichita was more than three miles from the Ryuns' house. But the campus of Southeast High sprawled only a few hundred yards away. Mrs. Ryun wanted her younger son to go to Southeast. But James wanted to attend East in order to take a special vocational course. His brother, Jerry, had gone to East for the same reason, and the mechanical drawing teacher at Curtis, Mr. Clifton, urged Jim to do so, too. (And he called the boy Jim, making Mrs. Ryun uncomfortable because she didn't like the sound of the nickname.)

Later, Jim learned that college-entrance kids at East sometimes looked down at the Vocational-school "Vokies." He was glad to go to East, though. He felt happy and eager on the bright September afternoon when new students gathered in the auditorium for their sophomore orientation assembly.

"A lot of you boys may have done poorly in junior-high sports," James heard a short, bright-eyed man telling the group. "You shouldn't be discouraged by that. Someday you may be a lot bigger and stronger than those fellows you competed against in eighth and ninth grade."

James listened closely. The speaker leaning against the stage was Bob Timmons, coach of East High's track and cross-country teams.

"Remember," Timmons went on, "no two boys grow at the same rate. Some of you still have a lot of growing to do. It's possible you'll never be built for football. If not, too bad. There's no way you can change that. But if you're healthy and you're a good student who is willing to work and who takes pride in a job well done, we want you to come out for cross-country. We think you might find it rewarding."

Cross-country? Jim Ryun wasn't sure what it was all about. It was something like track, wasn't it? After all, Mr. Timmons coached both sports. Of course, Jim didn't really expect to accomplish much in track, but he was going to try it next spring anyhow. So why not find out about cross-country? That afternoon, Jim reported to the field house behind East High's vocational-education building. "If I had known they made you run two miles in cross-country," he admitted later, "I probably never would have gone out for it."

The first day wasn't bad. The huge group jogged up a side street to the gentle slopes of College Hill Park for a long workout. The next morning when Jim sleepily climbed out of bed to make the rounds of his *Wichita Eagle* paper route, his legs felt so stiff and sore that he could hardly stand up.

Coach Timmons kept detailed records on his runners. But several weeks went by before he made any special notations on the bony sophomore with the awkward, head-wobbling style. As a matter of fact, Ryun's performance was so undistinguished that the coach didn't bother to learn the proper spelling of Jim's name. More than once in early September, he jotted down "Jim Ryan" or "Bill Ryun." On September 7, Jim was officially clocked for the first time in the mile run. Because his pace was so slow he needed more than four minutes to complete only three laps. Ryun's total time for the mile was 5:38, which he knew wasn't good enough to make the B team. He told himself that he would just have to work harder.

The keen competition at East High kept everyone working hard. During his next time trial, with a half-mile remaining, Jim and another B-team candidate started to sprint at the same time, each determined to shake the other. They raced shoulder to shoulder, neither willing to weaken, until they sped past a grove of pine trees and Ryun finally realized that he was running alone. His opponent had dropped back. Jim was elated. Although few of the other runners were aware of the little battle and Coach Timmons wasn't watching, it proved something to Jim Ryun. His legs felt as light as his heart when he finished the race that day.

On the following Monday, Ryun ran his two-mile time trial in 11:51. He was walking toward the locker room when Don Walker of the A team came up to him, smiling. "Good going, Ryun," Walker said. "That time of yours today is as fast as I ever did when I was a sophomore last year, and here you're running it in the third week of practice."

Pleased and surprised that a varsity runner had noticed him, Jim mumbled shyly, "Thanks. Uh, thanks a lot."

In the North High invitational meet at Echo Hills Golf Club, the fast-improving Ryun lowered his time to 11:23 and placed fourth in the B competition. A week later, the team took its first long road trip. For the entire 197-mile journey to the Shawnee Mission Invitational, Ryun sat wordlessly in the back of the station wagon, thinking and worrying. He was quiet on the return trip, too. But he was happy. Running against 90 other boys, Ryun had won the B race.

Coach Timmons was happy that day, too, and even happier two days later when Ryun earned a place on the A team. Jim simply clung to the heels of his new friend, Don Walker, who stepped up his own pace in an effort to shake the ambitious sophomore. In the last 80 yards of the two-mile test, Ryun swung wide, charged ahead of Walker and kept on sprinting until he passed long-legged varsity runner Chris Forsberg just before the finish line.

"Hey, coach," panted the amazed Forsberg. "How do you like that Ryun? He tied me."

Ryun blushed and said nothing. Timmons grinned. "Who're you kidding, Chris?" The coach chuckled. "Ryun beat you."

Then Timmons checked his stopwatch and grinned again. Ryun's time for the two-mile test was 10:36, almost a minute faster than he had ever run before.

After that, Timmons set progressively harder goals for his surprising sophomore. Still, the ungainly Ryun continued to amaze him. Jim swiftly worked his way to the top of Timmons' A-squad list. In the final meet of the year, at Emporia, Ryun's sixth-place finish led Wichita East to the state championship by a margin of two points over Wyandotte of Kansas City.

"Now that your season is finished, I hope we'll be seeing a little bit more of you, James," said his mother. Jim knew she was only half-joking when she used that tone of voice. The Ryuns were busy, and there was little enough time for family life. Mr. Ryun worked a night shift at Boeing Aircraft and Mrs. Ryun sold dresses at Sears Roebuck. Young Jim had both morning and evening paper routes. But if Mrs. Ryun thought her son was about to relax and enjoy himself now that the cross-country season was over, she was making a mistake.

3

I'd Like to be a Miler

Jim Ryun felt strange and self-conscious. The cold, gray December dawn didn't bother him so much; a newsboy got used to the early morning chill. But a roadside in Arkansas City, Kansas, was a peculiar place for a Wichita boy to find himself at 5:30 A.M., and a 50-mile hike was an even more peculiar reason for being there. "Come on, Ryun," jibed Jim's buddy, Chuck Sanders. "Entering this thing was your idea, wasn't it?"

Jim nodded sheepishly. "I must have been out of my mind," he muttered.

At first, hiking 50 miles to win a set of barbells had sounded like pure fun. It would be good practice for his running, and he wanted the weights so he could build up the muscles of his upper body for track. Of course, he and Chuck would win. As the day of the hike neared, however, Jim changed his mind. Chuck had' to convince him that the hike was still a good idea. Somehow, it hadn't occurred to Jim that other hikers in the group might think he and Chuck were a couple of fresh young show-offs. Now it was too late and a radio announcer from Wichita was chattering into a microphone and a crowd of shivering onlookers had gathered at the starting line. Jim just wanted to get away from the stares and set off on the long road back to Wichita.

The two 15-year-old boys in blue jeans started the hike at a rapid trot. They weren't showing off. They meant to run most of the way, if they could. But a burly walker in a mackinaw bellowed after them, "Hey, you kids, you think you're running the 100-yard dash or something?"

Ryun snickered in embarrassment. He knew his running style looked ridiculous. His left arm was free, but his right hand stayed jammed in the folds of his hooded sweat shirt, where it kept two apples and three candy bars from bouncing out on the highway. As he jogged along, he kept changing hands on the "lunch." Occasionally an oncoming car or truck whizzed past, its driver peering curiously at the boys. Traffic became more frequent as the morning wore on. The two young travelers alternately walked and ran, plodding steadily past the fields, farmhouses and barns of the Arkansas River valley. After a while, the well-conditioned boys found boredom almost as deadly as fatigue. It was a relief to reach the village of Oxford, where startled morning shoppers shook their heads in wonderment.

Before noon, Jim and Chuck reached Mulvane, the approximate mid-point of their trip. On the open road again, they flicked the dial of Chuck's transistor radio to KLEO, the Wichita station that was sponsoring the hike. A news bulletin reported that one of the station's own disc jockeys was setting a torrid pace in the trek from "Ark City" to Wichita. According to a later bulletin, the disc jockey was tiring but plugging bravely along at the head of the pack; he was clipping off the miles at what appeared to be a winning pace.

"Hey, we're so far ahead they've lost track of us," said Jim.

"Maybe we'd better take it easy," replied Chuck. "If there's nobody at the finish line to meet us when we get to Wichita, how will we collect the barbells?"

That was a problem the boys didn't have to solve. Roadside spectators began phoning the station. Before long, an official car cruised up behind the two teen-agers and confirmed that they were about six miles ahead of the supposedly front-running disc jockey. Dutifully, KLEO corrected its mistake.

Gerald Ryun leaped out of his easy chair after hearing the corrected announcement on his living room radio. "Mother," he said excitedly into the telephone, "I'll pick you up at the store in a few minutes. James and the Sanders boy are getting near the end of that

50-mile hike already and they're expected at the city limits a few minutes after dark. Let's get out there to meet them."

Mr. and Mrs. Ryun stood by proudly while their son was interviewed on the radio for the first time. ". . . And are you a runner at East High, Jim?" asked the announcer. Jim's mother winced when she heard the nickname.

"Yes, I hope to compete in track," she heard him say quietly. It was just like James not to mention what he had accomplished in cross-country. And it was like him, too, to add almost wistfully, "I'd like to be a miler."

The winter of 1962-1963 was mild in Wichita. When snow fell, it usually melted fast. But it couldn't melt fast enough for Jim Ryun. Two or three afternoons a week, Jim and Don Walker eagerly pulled on their sweat suits and training shoes, then romped through workouts on the city streets and crusty slopes of College Hill Park. One day Jim stopped at a downtown discount house and bought a cheap stopwatch. He took it along on his next cold, lonely workout over the East High track and clocked himself for a mile in 4 minutes, 40 seconds.

Coach Timmons hid his delight when the pleased sophomore told him about the 4:40 mile. Talking to the self-doubting Jim Ryun, of course, made it easy for the coach to mask his feelings. "Are you sure the watch was OK, Jim?" asked Timmons innocently.

"Gee, I think so," Jim said. Inwardly, he formed exactly the resolve Timmons was hoping for. He would show the coach. He would run the mile even faster.

East High's first track meet of the 1963 season fell on a bad day for the underweight tenth-grader. He couldn't shake off a cough that had bothered him all week. Teammate Chris Forsberg, who had outrun the feverish Ryun in the team interclass meet, was Timmons' main hope in the mile at the South High Invitational. Five points for first place were beyond Timmons' reasonable hopes, anyway, as long as state champion Charlie Harper of Wichita North was running the race. But Timmons hoped that Forsberg and Gerry Flanagan, both lettermen, might offset Harper's five points by taking second and third.

The morning of the meet was cold and gray, anything but cheerful for the first day of spring. Jim gulped cough syrup along with his breakfast. At lunch he was too nervous to swallow much besides his medicine. Harper's reputation as state champion wasn't responsible for Ryun's jittery feeling, though. Jim was barely conscious of whom he was running against. He was simply worried about his own showing. "I don't know why I feel this way," he said to himself, "but I'm scared silly of losing."

When the race began, Jim fell into stride automatically behind the boy in the red jersey. Numbly, he remained there as the laps clicked off—one, two, three—but as Harper increased speed for the final

Jim's mother often warmed up his dinner after he came home late from practice.

dash to the tape, Ryun mechanically stepped up his own pace. They crossed the line only a few inches apart, Harper the winner in a fast 4:32.2, Ryun just off his right shoulder, only two-tenths of a second behind.

That night Jim and his family saw the race televised on the 10:20 news report. Jim felt a little guilty for getting such a kick out of his own performance, but he couldn't help being excited. He made up his mind that Harper wasn't going to beat him next time.

"James, do you really think you're strong enough for all this running?" his mother asked. "You looked so terribly weak and tired after that race. And there are nights when you barely touch your dinner any more, dragging in here after all that practice. I'm really very worried."

Her husband was worried, too, but he respected the discipline and training required by track. He reassured his wife. "It's something the boy wants to do very badly, dear. Let him alone and we'll see what happens."

Jim's mother and sister were careful not to leave Jim completely alone, though. They soon fell into the habit of warming up his dinner each night when he came home late from practice, long after the rest of the family had eaten.

East High's own invitational meet was scheduled for the following week. "Jim, all of us think you can beat Harper," Gerry Flanagan insisted. Jim didn't admit it, but he thought so, too. The state champion himself devoted very little thought to the intense East High sophomore. He felt that if one loss wasn't enough to convince Ryun, another would be sure to do so.

Jim waited nervously for the day of the meet. Soon after the race began, he found himself dogging the heels of the fleet Harper. Throughout the second and third laps, Harper's fast pace failed to dislodge him. But as the runners sped down the backstretch of the fourth and final lap, the effects of the pace began to tell on Jim. On the next-to-last straightaway, Harper lengthened his stride and gradually pulled away. Ryun felt that he just couldn't make his legs move any faster.

"Darn it, he's going to beat me again," he thought as his rival, now almost 15 yards ahead, swung into the final turn. "And I really thought I was going to beat him. I worked so hard in practice. I worked so hard."

Grimly, Ryun realized there were still 110 yards between Charlie Harper and victory. If he had almost killed himself in practice, he might as well complete the job here and now. The pain in his chest, the weight in his thighs would be gone in a few seconds, anyway.

Harper heard the screaming of the fans, but doubted that a challenge was possible. Ryun had seemed thoroughly worn out after three-and-a-half laps. Could he still have the strength for a stretch kick? Then behind him, Harper heard the sound of footsteps, repeating the warning first sounded by the crowd. In disbelief and dismay, he turned his head just enough to glimpse the awkward, blue-jerseyed Ryun gallop wildly past—spraddle-legged and wobbly-headed—and hurl himself into the taut twine. As East High teammates swarmed around the exhausted Ryun, Harper groped for his hand and mumbled, "Nice race." The other East boys closed the circle around Ryun again, shaking his hand and pounding his back. In the second mile race of his young career, Jim Ryun had come from behind to upset the Kansas state high-school champion.

The next day, every copy of the *Wichita Eagle* that Jim tossed to his customers carried his picture

and his name in headlines. Almost guiltily, he stopped
to read Oren Campbell's by-lined article for the third
time:

> Sophomore Jim Ryun of East overtook North's de-
> fending state champion Charles Harper in the last
> 50 yards and beat him to the finish line by two
> strides, setting a meet mile record of 4 minutes,
> 26.4 seconds. Ryun . . . stayed on the North star's
> heels throughout the race until he sprinted past him
> at the finish. Ryun's time was seven-tenths of a
> second faster than the mark that was registered by
> former East sensation Archie San Romani Jr. in
> 1959.

Archie San Romani was somebody Ryun didn't
think about much. Coach Timmons thought about
him, though. While Ryun was working out early
the following week, Timmons drew him aside and
pointed to his clipboard.

"Look at this, Jim," he urged. "It's a chart of your
performances this year along with Archie's while he
was a sophomore here. You see his best time as a
sophomore? It was 4:26.5. You've already beaten that
and the season has barely started. Now look at this.
By the time Archie was a senior, he was running the
mile in 4:10. Do you get what I'm driving at?"

Jim said he wasn't sure. Timmons gazed at him
levelly.

"I'm talking about the four-minute mile, Jim. No
high school boy has ever run it. Don't you see? You

can be the first. If you're willing to work for it, I know you can do it."

Ryun looked at the coach incredulously. Only nine years earlier, England's Roger Bannister had become the first runner in history to crack the four-minute barrier.

"Me run a mile in four minutes?" Jim's voice cracked. "Coach, you must be crazy."

Some of Ryun's teammates thought so, too. At the East squad's next "Timmie talk"—the boys' private name for their earnest coach's discussion meetings —guffaws and giggles greeted the coach's announcement that the 15-year-old tenth grader was undertaking a special training program aimed at breaking the four-minute mile.

"You'll have to get used to people making fun of you," Timmons warned Jim later. "For a boy with your personality, that may be even harder than all the work this program will require. But that's the way it's going to be, because you're trying something nobody your age has ever tried before. I admit I don't know how this timetable of mine will work out, but we'll just have to adjust things as we go along. Neither of us will know until you get into it. That's the really tough part of it, Jim. You're out there all by yourself."

In his next meet, Jim won again. His time was 4:21.7. Then he beat Charlie Harper again, and the *Wichita Eagle* noted:

East's Ryun discarded his previous tactic of letting
. . . Harper set the pace. He led for all of the final
three laps, owning a three-yard lead the second time
around, five yards on the third lap and sprinting to
a 10-yard victory.

Newspapers in other Kansas towns also began to
write about Ryun. The following weekend, the two-
day Kansas Relays would be held on the rolling 900-
acre campus of the University of Kansas, in Lawrence, and the mile promised to be an eye-catcher.
In addition to Harper and Ryun the field would in-
clude the state cross-country champion, dark-haired
Tom Yergovich of Kansas City Wyandotte, and little
Gene McClain of Salina, a junior who had been timed
at 4:24 in his own sophomore season. In their col-
ums, the sports writers pointed out that any one of
the four could win, although Ryun had previously
beaten Yergovich by clocking 4:21.7 in the Wash-
ington-Bethel Relays. They also observed that Ryun's
rivalry with his hometown foe, Harper, seemed to be
turning into a one-sided affair.

The day of the meet was cloudless but breezy.
Ryun felt more jittery than ever. If he should lose to
any of the boys he had beaten earlier, he thought, it
would be an embarrassment, almost a disgrace. And
he wondered why nerves didn't seem to bother
McClain, the confident speedster in the dark-red
Salina uniform.

Approaching the finish line during the 1963 Kansas Relays, Ryun holds off the vainly struggling Yergovich.

After the start of the race, all the runners stayed tightly bunched for most of the first lap. Ryun reminded himself nervously that he couldn't afford to let himself be boxed in. Suddenly he bolted free of the pack like a frightened fawn, swung two lanes wide, made a swift charge and took first place. The crowd in the concrete stadium excitedly applauded the early display of speed.

Yergovich, startled, quickly closed the gap and settled into stride behind Ryun. McClain raced along outside of Yergovich. Harper fell back to fourth position, on the pole. The other starters dropped back. Until the final lap, the four favorites clung together in the same order. Suddenly Ryun was conscious of Yergovich, who was trying to move past on his right. Jim sped up. Both continued to pick up speed. They sprinted most of the last 220 yards, but at the finish line Yergovich was still struggling vainly, trying to brush past the stubborn Ryun. Jim's winning time was 4:21.3. Yergovich was clocked in 4:21.9, Harper in 4:23 and McClain in 4:24.4. It was a marvelously fast, finely contested high-school mile, and the cheers of the thousands of fans at KU were loud and long.

For a long time after the race, the victor was too tired to talk to the reporters. "How old is Jim Ryun?" they asked. "How long has he been running? How did he get so fast all of a sudden?"

Proudly, Timmons took over. "Jim knows the value of hard work," he told the sports writers. "The first time this youngster ran a mile last fall, he finished fourteenth and we timed him in 5:38. What was he today, a minute and seventeen seconds faster? That's hard to believe, isn't it?" The reporters scratched busily on their note pads. "I don't know how good Jim is going to be," Timmons went on. "He won't even be sixteen until next week. He still doesn't have good speed. But he wins because he can still run while all the other boys are tired."

The next day Timmons assigned Ryun to run the last leg of the two-mile relay for East. Yergovich and Harper were anchor men for their teams in the same race. This time, of course, the familiar rivals were running an unfamiliar distance—a half-mile. Wyandotte's third runner passed the baton to Yergovich while Ryun and Harper were still waiting for the arrival of their teammates. But Ryun made up the distance, stretched out at the finish, and won the race for Wichita East.

A week later, in the Hutchinson Invitational, Jim won his fifth straight mile, this time by almost 150 yards. The competition wasn't close because Charlie Harper didn't run the mile. Instead, he had switched to the 880-yard run, or half-mile.

In the Kansas State meet at Wichita University, Ryun officially took over the mile title that had belonged to Harper a year earlier. Ryun won it convincingly. He outran McClain, Harper and the lame Yergovich, who had twisted an ankle three days before the meet. His margin of victory was 12 yards and his time was 4:16.2, which broke Archie San Romani's Kansas high-school record.

"No, I have no idea of Jim Ryun's ultimate potential," coach Timmons told the Kansas City sports writers as they pressed him for more information on his East High prodigy. "But it looks like the only way we'll find out is for Jim to run against the college boys."

Exactly a week later, Jim did.

4

The Kid at Compton

The mile and half-mile races in the Missouri Valley Amateur Athletic Union (AAU) meet at Kansas City would take place at night, and they were scheduled to start about an hour and 45 minutes apart. Jim Ryun was listed to run in both. As he warmed up under the floodlights, sloshing through puddles formed by an afternoon rain, he tried not to think about the second race. A mile against older runners would be hard work enough for one night.

As it turned out, the pace of that mile was almost enough to discourage him completely. Every time Jim increased his speed in an attempt to pass Wichita University's star miler, Cal Elmore, the college runner held him off with an added burst. Elmore tore into the last lap so strongly that he began to edge away from Ryun, and Jim knew that it would be impossible to catch him. He could only keep forcing himself on. He made a brave try and the crowd rewarded him with a big hand. Jim's time was a fine 4:08.2, but at the finish he was about 18 yards behind.

"A real good effort, Jim," said Timmons. Jim's stomach heaved uncontrollably. He felt sick and downhearted.

"Coach," he said, struggling into his sweat suit, "I couldn't run again tonight if my life depended on it. Let's forget the 880."

Timmons could see it was an effort for the youngster to talk. "We'll just wait and see," he replied calmly. Then he walked away. Later, he returned and advised Jim to try limbering up. Jim shook his head wearily, but stood and stretched his muscles. Before long he was jogging down the backstretch. Soon, in spite of himself, he was willing to race again.

The half-mile proved to be painful and Jim was beaten again. In fact, he finished fifth—the sort of losing effort he had almost forgotten. Again, however, his time of 1:54.5 was faster than his previous best half-mile. It was easy to see that Timmons was delighted. This kind of progress was important, and his insistence that Jim try the "double" had proved something to both of them. Yet Jim asked himself seriously if the effort had been worth it. The value of extra and often discouraging effort would not become apparent until much later in his career.

Jim's parents were already in bed when he got home long after midnight. He was too tired to wake them. He went quietly to bed and immediately fell asleep. At breakfast the next morning, Mr. and Mrs. Ryun asked eagerly for details of the meet.

"I lost both races," Jim answered simply. "I finished second in the mile and fifth in the half-mile." That was all he wanted to say.

"You'll do better next time, dear," said his mother helpfully.

Jim did, too. He ran the half-mile in a regional meet and although he finished behind four college runners, he lowered his time again. His 1:53.6 was the fastest time ever recorded for the half-mile distance by a Kansas high-school boy.

The next step in Timmons' plans called for Jim to try another mile in fast competition, at the United States Track and Field Federation meet in Houston, Texas. Jim had never made a trip as long as the 514-mile journey to Houston. He bought a new suit. The coach had decided to travel by train, in the hope that the ride might give the boy a chance to relax. Hour after hour, Jim sat silently, watching the trees and telegraph wires slip past the train window. Timmons watched him uneasily, wondering what to do or say as a distraction. He could think of nothing.

In the meet at Houston's Jeppesen Stadium, Jim overcame his nervousness early in the race. He finished sixth in 4:07.8. The winner of the race was Cal Elmore, whose time was 4:02.2. It took Jim almost a half-hour to get over his terrible nausea and dizziness.

Afterward, while watching Jim's post-race "warm-down," Timmons mused over the mental struggle he knew the boy was enduring. Jim obviously didn't realize the extent of his abilities. He still thought like a lonely high-school kid and not like the four-minute miler he actually was. At 16, Jim was already good enough to buck the best miler in the country, but the problem was to convince him of that. The coach had entered Jim in the National AAU meet to be held in St. Louis, but the boy felt that he didn't belong among such stiff competition. At a result, Timmons had to think of some way to get him ready for the AAU meet and a mile against Jim Beatty, who had just run a 3:55.5 mile for an American record.

Timmons was spared that problem. While working out in his bare feet at the McDonald golf course one afternoon, Jim stepped on a broken pop bottle and slashed his right foot. Reluctantly, Timmons canceled the trip to St. Louis. As for Jim, he just felt relieved. He still lacked the confidence in himself that Timmons obviously felt. He was afraid that running against Beatty and the other strong runners he knew by reputation might destroy whatever belief he held in his own ability. But as soon as the foot healed, he started working harder than ever.

Each morning of summer vacation, he rose at 5:30 and set out on a five-mile run. The drivers of trucks rumbling along Kellogg Avenue at dawn frequently saw Jim's lean figure racing alongside the highway past the stores and used-car lots of Wichita's east side. They never imagined how long and how far he would keep running, or that he would be back at it again that same evening, running another six or seven miles.

To relieve the monotony of those long runs, Jim sometimes ran out into the country and loped along the dusty country roads and across the grassy fields. He was pleased when Timmons told him he had entered several of the boys in something called an "Olympic Development" meet at Independence, Missouri, in July. Jim would be running in the three-mile event. That, at least, was something to shoot for, and it would be a break in the routine. Even though he was running in a different event, he would have a chance to measure his progress.

The trip to Independence took four hours. When Jim and the other runners from the Wichita Track Club arrived at the meet site, they wanted to turn around and go home. There were no spectators, and only one bored-looking official appeared. The cinder track was so rough and scraggly that it had probably never been rolled. Jim's original goal had been to run the three miles in 14:30, but he ran half-heartedly. Although he set an age-group record with a clocking of 14:53, he felt disgusted with the indifferently-staged meet. Timmons was unhappy, too, but for different reasons.

"Jim, you slacked off," the coach told him impatiently. "Just because you have enough ability to get

As a runner in training at East High, Ryun had to be careful of his diet.

by, you think you can take it easy sometimes. That's a bad attitude. It's a bad habit. If you want to accomplish anything at all next year, you can't ease up. You've got to work as hard as you're able."

Jim resented the lecture. How hard did other runners work, after all? A few months later Timmons scolded him again. Pizza-burgers had been on the lunch menu in the East High cafeteria one day, and Jim had gulped down several of the highly seasoned meat patties. That afternoon his stomach had ached so much that he was forced to drop out of a cross-country time trial.

"You've got to remember what you're trying to accomplish," the coach reminded him sternly. "You can't have merely winning as a goal. If you do, you'll slip back. You've got to run against time, and the watch is a tough competitor."

Timmons knew that a great deal more than high-school competition would be necessary to bring out Ryun's best efforts. Jim was undefeated that autumn in high-school meets, but Timmons also entered him in an AAU meet at Kansas City. In that race, four miles long, he finished third.

After the end of the season, the coach provided another incentive. He entered Jim in his first indoor meet. One of his opponents in a special two-mile run at the San Francisco Cow Palace was an equally ambitious high-school athlete, little Gerry Lindgren of Spokane, Washington. The prospect of running on the unfamiliar banked boards disturbed Jim, and he practiced daily in the field house at Wichita State University, running sprints on the concrete-based floor. His concern over the indoor conditions increased when Don Walker jokingly told him, "If you think the boards are tough, wait till you sniff the air in there. All the cigar smokers like to sit right next to the track at indoor meets and they fill the place with smoke."

Walker was only kidding, of course, but his playful comment added to Jim's worries. On the night of the race, as he stood in front of a crowd of 12,117, he was quite jittery. The start was rough. Someone jostled

Jim and he lost his balance. While Lindgren and the other runners dashed away, the Wichita youngster stumbled off the track. By the time he got up and started to run, the race seemed to be a lost cause. Jim needed every bit of his drive and determination to make up most of the ground he had lost. Eventually he passed every rival except Lindgren, but he lost count of the laps and, instead of speeding up for a final burst on his last official lap, he plodded steadily past the finish line and continued around the track again. The extra lap, of course, did not count, and by saving his sprint for it, Jim lost the chance to shorten his time on what should have been his concluding lap. He finished in 9:22.6.

Jim's twice-a-day workouts became more difficult after winter arrived. One dark, freezing morning, instead of going out into the snow, he rolled over and went back to sleep. This short break in his training schedule made him feel so guilty that he got up promptly the next morning and pushed himself through a harder workout. Breakfast on those wintry days was a thermos jug of tomato soup and two peanut butter sandwiches, gulped on the run before his first class at East High.

Timmons tried to lend encouragement. But the State of Kansas has strict rules governing the amount of time spent together by coaches and their athletes between seasons. Besides, much of Timmons' time was taken up by his duties as swimming coach. Don Walker tried to accompany Jim on his workouts at least once a day, but found the effort very tiring, especially when added to his own paper route. The slippery, sloshy running made it even worse. "I don't know how you keep it up," Walker marveled.

Gradually, Jim's rigorous program increased his strength and stamina. By spring, high-school rivals had learned that there was little hope of beating him at any distance. For several weeks he had to stop training because of a bad cold and a growth in his throat. Still, the goal of the four-minute mile kept him going. In the state meet at Kansas State's Memorial Stadium, Jim set such a murderous pace that there was nobody close to him after the first two laps. He galloped home 70 yards ahead in 4:06.4, a national high-school record. And in spite of the fact that he had no competition to speak of, he pushed himself so hard that he needed almost a half-hour to recover. When he confessed he had never been so tired after a race, rivals found it hard to believe.

"Man, that was no high-school pace," said Gene McClain in awe. "I figured on running 4:10 today, but I didn't come close to it. You burned me out trying to keep up with you. I wouldn't have beaten you, anyway, but I would've come a lot closer if I'd just hung back and minded my own business."

Now, even if Jim himself remained uncertain, others knew he was ready to run against the best. He was invited to run the mile in nationally publicized meets at Modesto and Compton, California. Between classes, students at East High collected $121 to help

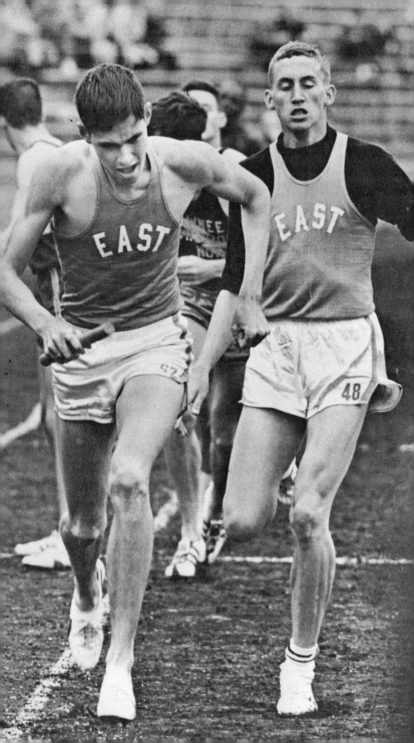

pay Ryun's and Timmons' expenses to the Modesto Relays.

"I'm pretty scared about the competition, but I'm pretty happy about being invited," Jim told his schoolmates gratefully. Timmons knew Jim would be nervous, facing such outstanding milers as Tom O'Hara and Dyrol Burleson. On the plane trip west he advised him, "On the first three laps, don't worry about the leaders. Just try to keep in contact with the fourth and fifth runners. Then run the last lap as fast as you can."

Jim nodded. A stewardess stopped to talk to the coach about Jim, and the boy listened in embarrassment. He realized what an honor it was to run against the country's best milers, but it bothered him to hear someone talk about it.

At Modesto, Timmons was even more conscious than Jim that some of the better runners—and their coaches—were resentful of the youngster's presence. Meet officials, too, made it plain that they did not rate the teen-ager nearly as high as his opponents in the mile.

Timmons asked the officials to place a timer at the 1,500-meter mark because Jim would be trying to break Archie San Romani's high-school record. The coach wanted to know Jim's time for both the 1,500-meters and the mile. Of course, that would have required an additional timer, who would be stationed 118 yards short of the finish line for the mile to record the boy's clocking for the shorter metric distance.

Ryun takes the baton from Chris Forsberg during the 1964 Kansas Relays.

Modesto officials refused. "We're only taking split times for the better runners," Timmons was told.

The coach had an even greater worry on his mind, however. He feared that Jim, remembering his race against Gerry Lindgren, would try too hard to avoid trouble at the start in Modesto. Sure enough, Jim started in Lane Six and immediately dropped back behind the others. Even worse, Jim seemed so rattled that he didn't maintain the pace they had planned. Still running eighth, he finished the first lap in 63 seconds, more than four seconds behind schedule.

"Move up, Jim, move up," muttered the coach. But Jim was still last at the half-mile. Suddenly he seemed to snap awake. On the backstretch of the third lap, Timmons saw his young runner move abruptly past two rivals and charge ahead toward the leaders. There was no hope of Ryun hearing a familiar voice in that huge, noisy crowd, but Timmons couldn't help shouting.

The red-headed O'Hara began his sprint with a full 330 yards still to go. Timmons saw that Ryun, too, was sprinting hard. Burleson, amazingly fresh, swept past Ryun in the stretch and dueled O'Hara to the wire. The order of finish was Burleson, O'Hara, Ryun. The winning time was 4:00.2 and Ryun's third-place clocking was 4:01.7.

In voting for the outstanding performance of the meet, sports writers gave the most support to Ralph Boston, a veteran long jumper who reached his career peak with a leap of 27 feet, $2\frac{1}{2}$ inches. Second, only

*Whenever Jim competed out of town his father would take over his
paper route. Here he prepares his son's papers for delivery.*

three votes behind, was the high-school kid from
Kansas, Jim Ryun.

"Hello, there, Jim Ryun," a familiar voice greeted
him as he boarded the Continental Airlines jet for
the first leg of the return flight to Wichita. It was the
same cute stewardess who had served them on the
outgoing flight. "How was your race?" she asked
pleasantly. "Where did you finish?"

Jim blushed. "Only third," he said.

After a five-hour delay in Denver, Jim and Timmons boarded their plane for Wichita. As the aircraft taxied to a stop outside the Wichita terminal, they could see a big crowd gathering at the gate. It was a reception for Jim. The boy snapped shut the case for his reading glasses, glanced uncomfortably out at the crowd and swallowed hard. "Here comes the hardest part of the trip," he murmured.

All Wichita seemed proud of their native son. Jim's parents were kept busy for the next few days answering the telephone, thanking friends and strangers for their interest. The Wichita City Commission issued a proclamation, wishing Jim Ryun success "in his goal to break the four-minute mile."

By this time, Jim had cut down his running to seven or eight miles a day. He was working mainly for speed. One morning, as a steady downpour drenched Wichita and submerged the East High track, Jim, undismayed, put on his low-cut sneakers and a rain-proof jacket. Then he splashed off for his daily workout through the streets of the city.

Ryun knew exactly what he wanted to accomplish in his next race at Compton. The same strong opponents he had faced at Modesto would be there—Burleson, O'Hara and Cary Weisiger. So would Jim Grelle, Morgan Groth and Timmons' earlier East High protégé, the University of Oregon's Archie San Romani. But foremost in Jim's mind was his familiar, implacable foe, the clock. None of the insistent newsmen knew; none of Jim's friends and schoolmates knew; none of the nation's track fans—suddenly conscious of the teen-age wonder from Wichita—had any way of knowing the personal goal Ryun was setting for Compton: a 3-minute, 59-second mile.

The race at Compton started so fast that it looked like a sprint. The track was in ideal shape and the crowd of 7,750 sensed from the beginning that the race would be an exciting one. Jim fought to get a good position on the first turn and managed to come out of the tangled pack in second place. Burleson was close behind him, he knew, and so was O'Hara. There were many fast, powerful runners in the field. Jim strained to hear the voice of the clockers as he flashed past them in third position at the end of the opening lap. His time was good, just over 59 seconds. On the next lap, he allowed several runners to glide smoothly past him. The important thing was to maintain a good, strong pace. At the 880 mark, he was still satisfied—2:01 and a fraction.

To the crowd, the race still resembled a mob scene. The leaders jockeyed continually for position, and most of the followers clung stubbornly to the pace. Heading into the home stretch for the next-to-last time, Jim felt a jarring thump, and then he was stumbling off the track, losing valuable time. If only they'd just let him run, he thought as he regained the track. Most of his opponents were older and stronger. He always seemed to be using precious energy trying to avoid collisions and stay on his feet.

The near-spill left him trailing most of the runners in the race and lagging behind his own timetable as well. The last lap was a blurring, all-out drive that left him still far back in the pack, barely conscious at the finish.

It seemed curious to Jim that so many fans wanted his autograph. They thronged around, pressing programs into his hand and waving slips of paper. He signed as many as he could, wondering self-consciously if any of the other milers might be looking. After all, he had finished so dismally far back. Eighth place, wasn't that what someone told him?

The crowd hushed when the public address speakers broadcast an audible click from the microphone. "Ladies and gentlemen, official results of the mile run . . . First was Dyrol Burleson, 3 minutes, 57.4 seconds. Second was Tom O'Hara, 3 minutes, 57.6 seconds . . ." The voice droned on.

"By the time he gets to me," thought Jim in self-mockery, "that announcer will be out of breath."

". . . In seventh place, Cary Weisiger, 3 minutes, 58.9 seconds. And in eighth place, Jim Ryun, 3 minutes, 59 seconds flat."

Jim just couldn't believe his ears. And suddenly the spectators were cheering so loudly that it was hard to hear the booming voice of the announcer as he continued, "For the first time in the history of track and field, ladies and gentlemen, eight runners in the same race have broken four minutes in the mile. And here tonight, for the first time, a high-

Ryun (arrow) crossed the finish line with a time of exactly 3 minutes and 59 seconds to become the first high-school boy to break the four-minute barrier.

school boy has broken the four-minute barrier. Jim Ryun of Wichita, Kansas, becomes the first school-boy to run a mile in less than four minutes."

The next morning, it seemed as if the phone in Jim's hotel room would never stop buzzing. If all the long-distance callers were to be believed, every television set in central Kansas would be tuned that afternoon to Wichita's Channel 3 for the replay of the meet. Jim was overwhelmed by the fact that he had achieved a goal he once thought impossible. In only his second high-school track season, he had broken the four-minute mile.

Timmons, taking on reporter after reporter, recited the facts of Jim's life so often that he was able to anticipate almost every question. "I knew Jim had the capabilities," Timmons said. "But there's a lot of pressure on him now. All of a sudden he's in the national track spotlight and he's not so sure he likes it. This has been a strange experience for him, running against the top college and open milers in the country. From now on, he'll always be in danger of blowing up, because that pressure can reach him in any race."

It was natural for Timmons to look ahead. He knew that his young star was doing the same thing, shaping his thoughts around a new goal. As both of them realized, it was only four months until October, 1964, and the Olympic Games in Tokyo, Japan.

5

Fatigue is Pain

On May 6, 1954, Roger Bannister ran a mile in less than four minutes. He was the first man to do this. Later, he became a doctor in London. The more Bannister studied medicine, the more he learned about his own achievement—and the achievements of the faster runners who succeeded him. He concluded, "The longer the distance an athlete runs, the more important is will power and the less important is physique. Motivation is the key to it all."

When Dr. Bannister was told about Jim Ryun's tireless training, he commented, "Obviously [it] requires a single-minded dedication, even ruthlessness, that few athletes possess." Nobody who knew the self-doubting Kansas schoolboy would ever have called him ruthless. But single-minded? That he was.

Coach Timmons' training system for his runners included the use of a clock normally employed in timing swimmers.

It was relatively easy for a busy athlete to pass up the frequent visits that fellow students made to Armstrong's ice cream parlor, just across Douglas Avenue from Wichita East High. But it was very hard to get up early on cold winter mornings, to work twice a day and to run the way Ryun ran, until the habit was so strong that it became a part of his nature. In Bannister's time, barely ten years earlier, no coach had dared to work a teen-age athlete that hard. Bob Timmons was one of the first to realize that it could be done.

As a boy in Pittsburg, Kansas, Timmons had to make up for his own lack of size by trying harder in athletics. He served three years in the Marine Corps before finishing college at the University of Kansas and realizing his goal of coaching. From his experience as a swimming coach, he learned that modern swimmers must start at an early age. "They're too young to know it's work," Timmons said with a chuckle. "They think it's fun."

Timmons decided that teen-age trackmen could be trained just as intensively as young swimmers. After all, wasn't that the best way to learn their potential? Along with the work, Timmons gave his youngsters a method of measuring their progress.

"With individual goals," he explained, "each boy can find his own average speed and then compete to improve it. The goals have to depend on ability and potential, because if they're out of balance, a boy's interest in the sport will be destroyed. Too strong a desire to achieve a distant goal can ruin the pleasure and importance of day-to-day achievement. But when a boy's legs get tired, we can work on his arms, get him into another activity like weight lifting or calisthenics. That will also keep up his interest between meets and make training more fun."

Fun? The boys at East High snickered at the idea. Of course, they had to admit grudgingly that the Timmons system seemed to work. Every year, late in the season, newspapers in other Kansas cities would begin to call his track teams "the horrible horde from Wichita East" and "the seldom-beaten Blue Aces." Early-season meets didn't concern Timmons too much. Often, Ryun's more outspoken teammates grumbled when the coach pushed them through a hard practice on the day before one of these early meets.

"We don't point for meets until late in the year," Timmons told them patiently. "We point for the big meets—city, regional and state. Sure, you'll be tired in the early meets. You won't do as well as you might if you rested for a day or two beforehand. But by the time the 'goal meets' come along, you'll be ahead. You'll be running faster and stronger."

On the few occasions when Ryun wanted to relax his training efforts, it didn't help to hear teammates sympathizing with him or criticizing the coach. "Timmie takes all the fun out of it," they complained.

Some of them knew that Timmons' assistant, big, hearty J. D. Edmiston, also disagreed with the head coach at times. In private, Edmiston would argue, "Timmie, it doesn't make sense to wear out the shot putters and discus throwers and high jumpers with all this running the day before a meet."

To that, Timmons would reply, "I know we can't convince all the boys this is a sound system. Every athlete likes to achieve his best performance every time he competes. But what good is winning an early-season contest with a mediocre performance? That amounts to settling for something insignificant, instead of striving for something really worthwhile in the future."

Whenever Jim Ryun grew impatient with Timmie, he usually admitted to himself that the coach had taught him a great deal about worthwhile goals. By now, it was clear to the whole East High track team that Jim's developing talent and tremendous inner drive made him exceptional. He was a special case whom teammates found almost impossible to resent. Sometimes they even felt sorry for him.

In early 1964, Ryun's typical morning workout consisted of running five miles at an even pace—what Timmons called "striding." That same afternoon, after warming up, he would run ten fast half-miles, slowing to a quarter-mile jog between each 880, but never coming to a stop. Then he would finish off by striding another four-and-a-half miles.

Ryun listens thoughtfully as Timmons talks to the track team.

Only a former champion miler turned doctor—for example, Roger Bannister—could completely understand the demands made on Ryun's young body. It was the body of a skinny, 17-year-old boy who was still growing; a shy, unsure youngster, troubled by frequent colds and allergies; a youngster with an inner-ear ailment so serious that it affected his hearing and complicated his head-wobbling problem by making him dizzy.

Bannister, who had trained only 30 minutes a day while competing in track, also recognized the necessity for increasing a runner's oxygen supply through rigorous conditioning. Oxygen must be carried from the air to the muscles. The longer a person runs, the more oxygen he needs, and the more harmful lactic acid builds up in his body, filling his muscles with pain. Training enlarges his lungs, enlarges his heart and strengthens the muscles, enabling them to absorb more and more oxygen. The whole question was how much training a boy like Ryun could stand.

"I know I've been criticized about Jim's training," said Timmons. "But once the boy believes in the system as Jim does, the basic element is hard work. You just have to punch through the fatigue barrier. This is pain. To be a champion, you must be able to battle it. How would a baseball player, for example, or even a shot putter understand the awful pain Jim goes through?"

Several weeks before the race at Compton, Jim and his teammates had learned that Timmons would be leaving Wichita East to take a college job. The earnest little coach had been hired for the following year as assistant track coach at the University of Kansas, in Lawrence. In Ryun's senior year, popular J. D. Edmiston was going to coach the Blue Aces.

In the spring of 1964, however, Jim's senior year seemed far away. Instead, his thoughts, and those of Timmons, focused on Jim's "really worthwhile goal" —making the United States Olympic team.

The initial step in Jim's Olympic plans was his first half-mile against top-flight American competition. The emphasis was on speed. Setting a lofty goal of 1:48 for the 880 at San Diego, California, he placed fifth and ran 1:50.3, missing his target because he wilted in the last 220 yards.

A crowd of 200 students greeted Ryun and Timmons on their return to Wichita Municipal Airport. A police-escorted motorcade whisked them to East High for a special assembly in honor of Jim. Signs and banners proclaimed, "Welcome home, Champ," and "We are proud of you."

Jim was too modest, still too unsure of himself to answer all the questions from his schoolmates. Timmons, standing alongside him in front of the auditorium stage, answered most of them. But Jim managed to express his feelings.

"It feels good to enter rough competition as I have the past two weeks," he said. "I think it's the ambition of every athlete to make the Olympics, but I'm not counting on it yet. Probably the most important thing I've learned is to be on guard during the race so I don't get bumped off the track the way I did at Compton. Nobody does a thing like that on purpose. They're a great bunch of guys, and besides, they do all the work. I just let them set the pace and I try to keep up."

Step two was a Kansas "all-comers" meet in which Jim tried the two-mile event. The emphasis this time was on endurance. Jim ran a satisfactory 9:06.5.

The official Olympic trials were next on Jim's schedule, beginning with the National AAU meet on the Rutgers University track at New Brunswick, New Jersey. Ryun found himself listed in the same preliminary heat of the Olympic-distance 1,500-meters (exactly 118 yards, 9 inches shorter than a mile) as the favorite, Dyrol Burleson. It turned out to be a lucky break.

As usual, Burleson ran the first two laps back in the pack. He liked to let others do the pacesetting work. Ryun had to fall back behind Burleson in order to be sure of avoiding the early jam-up. On the third lap, he tried to move up, but found himself boxed in by a runner ahead of him and another to the side of him. Suddenly he heard the voice of the older, wiser Burleson just behind him, offering advice.

"Take it easy, now. Don't crowd the curb." Burleson's words came in little bursts of breath. "Just move out and stay with me. Stay with me and you'll be all right."

When Burleson moved, so did Ryun. They headed

into the fourth lap and pounded ahead toward a grassy hillside that was dotted with spectators. Burleson dashed all the way to the front and Ryun followed. The crew-cut Oregonian kept sprinting, with the youngster right on his heels, until they circled the track and crossed the line almost together. Burleson's time was 3:46.1, Ryun's 3:46.3.

Before the final race the next day, Burleson talked to Ryun, putting him at ease again. Burleson's calmness amazed Ryun. The important thing at this stage, Burleson pointed out, was passing the qualifying test. Winning didn't matter that much. Qualifying was also the chief goal of Jim Grelle. Realizing this, Ryun was satisfied to finish fourth the next day. All the first four finishers—O'Hara, Burleson, Grelle and Ryun—broke Cary Weisiger's three-week-old American record of 3:39.3 for the "metric mile" (1,500 meters). And Ryun was pleased to see that Burleson remained calm even though O'Hara had beaten him for the first time in seven races.

Burleson was so unflustered, in fact, that he surprised the sports writers who wanted to ask about his loss. Instead, he talked to them about Ryun. "That kid has so much talent," Burleson said, "that it scares me to think what he'll do when he gets going. What a future!" The reporters from the New York newspapers, racing to file their stories before a Sunday-evening deadline, tried to interview Ryun, but found the boy too tired to say much.

After a little rest, Jim was able to collect his

thoughts and analyze his performance for his own record. He realized that, in spite of pulling out far too wide for his final sprint, he had blazed home in 3:39 flat. That was good, very good, he thought. (Although he didn't know it at the time, his 3:39 would have been fast enough to win the gold medal in any previous Olympic 1,500-meters except that run by Australian Herb Elliott in Rome four years earlier. Elliott had won with a time of 3:35.6.)

Jim confided to Timmons, "I'm still scared, but it's not as bad as it used to be. I've run against Burleson and O'Hara three times now. I think maybe I have a chance."

At the following week's major Olympic trial in New York's Randall's Island Stadium, the heat was a stifling 94 degrees. The flush on Bob Timmons' face, however, came from pure pride. Ryun qualified for the final by placing third in a heat won by his familiar opponent from Wichita, Archie San Romani. Jim's time was 3:49.6.

The final was run on the Fourth of July. As he always seemed to, in a race against the nation's outstanding runners, Ryun ran scared. He looked so reluctant at the start that Timmons feared the whole Olympic effort had been in vain. Jim fell into stride at the very rear of the pack and remained last for two circuits of the track. The pace was slow. Burleson, O'Hara and the others were not trying to achieve record times. The important thing was to make the Olympic team. The New York meet would shave the 1,500-meter field to six men. Eventually, only three would win out.

As the jockeying continued on the third lap, with Burleson and O'Hara glancing at each other suspiciously, Ryun took a supercautious, long route to the outside and started to close the gap on the leaders. Now was the time for him to summon all the speed that the recent workouts had been intended to develop. Everything depended on the last-lap sprint, and the slow pace indicated that all the runners had plenty of strength left. The American Broadcasting Company's "Wide World of Sports" television camera swung swiftly, following the runners as they picked up speed. Suddenly announcer Jim McKay forgot the duel for first place.

"Look at that kid," he barked excitedly. "A high school junior—against two of the greatest milers in the world, O'Hara and Burleson."

To Ryun's amazement and delight, he found himself gaining with every stride. He felt full of wallop. Avoiding all contact with the others, he stayed wide on the track and flung himself forward, around the final turn and into the last straightaway, until he could see ahead of him the thin white string stretched across the track. As he strained to catch Burleson and O'Hara, he was conscious of deep-breathing, long-stepping Jim Grelle at his side. It was a blanket finish, the kind that always sends a crowd into roaring excitement. First, in 3:45.4, was Dyrol Burleson, aged 24. Second, in 3:45.6, Tom O'Hara, aged 22.

Third, in 3:46.1, was 27-year-old Jim Grelle. Fourth, in the same time as Grelle, was 17-year-old Jim Ryun. It was close enough to keep Ryun's chances alive, to give him a final chance to make the team.

The television camera quickly flicked from the grinning Burleson to the drawn, skinny Ryun, who was rolling his big, sad eyes in pain and bewilderment. Announcer McKay couldn't control his voice. It betrayed his astonishment. "You can see he's just a kid," he told the nationwide ABC audience incredulously. "He's just a plain old kid."

Ryun looked less like a frightened fawn by the time he appeared on the Los Angeles Coliseum track two months later for the final Olympic trials. He also had his first crew cut. Late that summer, Jim had gone to Lawrence to live with Timmons on a farm the coach had rented. There, the coach could supervise his workouts. As a result, his parents didn't see the new haircut for some time. But they needed no explanation for the loss of his long, wavy hair. Coach Timmons had a crew cut and so had Jim's idol, Dyrol Burleson.

Several days before the Los Angeles meet, Jim's picture appeared—with his new crew cut and in the gold uniform of the Wichita Kiwanis Track Club —on the cover of *Sports Illustrated* magazine. With all the publicity, he was embarrassed but not surprised to find himself one of the favorites of the crowd of 18,981 that turned out for the second day of the Los Angeles trials. Jim listened carefully to Timmons'

In the closely contested Olympic Trials in Los Angeles, both Ryun and Grelle (6) cross the 1,500-meter finish line in 3:41.9. The photo-finish cameras confirmed Ryun's third-place victory by inches.

final words of advice. For all they both knew, it might be the last tip the college-bound coach would ever offer him.

"Don't just run for the finish line," Timmons warned. "You can't afford any letup at the end. Run past the finish. Run as fast as you can until you're ten yards past it."

Jim meant to. Burleson's victory in New York

had all but assured him of a place on the United States team, and now only two 1,500-meter spots were open. In addition to Burleson, Ryun and four more sub-four-minute milers were in the race. In fact, from the beginning of the race all of them kept such close tabs on each other that, with less than 300 yards to go, the two Olympic berths remained open to all. Out wide went Ryun, two lanes wide this time, as he turned on his stretch kick. Burleson and O'Hara kicked hard, too. Just a whisker behind them sped Jim Grelle, sprinting desperately for the right to represent Uncle Sam in Japan.

Ryun forgot his coach's advice about running past the finish line. He forgot everything but Grelle. Ten yards from the finish, he edged even with Grelle and side by side they strained to squeeze ahead of one another. Ryun gathered his energy for a final lunge. Just as he launched it, Grelle threw himself forward toward the line across the cinders. They hit the finish only inches apart and Grelle, falling, sprawled on the track. Both were timed in 3:41.9, less than a second behind Burleson and O'Hara. But this time the judges agreed that Ryun was ahead. This was soon confirmed by the photo-finish cameras. The third United States runner in the Olympic 1,500-meters would be Jim Ryun.

The closing ceremonies in the massive Coliseum were a jumbled blur for the jubilant Ryun. First he posed for photographers. He tried to obey their instructions to form a smile by saying "Cheese." But

Jim marches proudly between O'Hara and Burleson in the parade of Olympic athletes.

after baring his teeth several times while saying "Cheese," the youngster decided on a happier word. "Tokyo," he repeated over and over as the cameras clicked and flashed.

Then he put on his gray sweat suit, answered newsmen's questions in front of a microphone and signed autographs. After that, he walked happily down the lime-lined track between O'Hara and Burleson in the parade of Olympic athletes.

Jim started his "warmdown" after the march of athletes. As the fans were leaving the stadium and the TV technicians began to pack up their equipment, Ryun jogged alone around the track for three laps.

J. D. Edmiston rescued Jim from another clawing pack of autograph hunters outside the Coliseum.

Tired, but too happy to notice it, Jim joined the Wichita delegation that included his two coaches, his mother and father, East High principal Sid Moore, television newsman Bob Kyle and businessman Waldo Leisy, who had flown to the West Coast in his private plane. It was the brightest day of Jim's life, and he was glad to share it with his family and friends. From now on, he was on his own. Members of the United States team were bound for Walnut, California, where they would train for two weeks before departing for Tokyo.

Since Jim was to be gone for more than a month, his father volunteered to take over the paper route back home in Wichita. His first day's deliveries made him immensely proud. The *Wichita Eagle* carried this editorial:

> Jim has found the secret of using a greater amount of his talent in the field of distance running. And that secret is plain hard work. Hopefully his achievement will be a model and symbol for other youngsters who have hidden potential—not particularly in track, but in many fields of endeavor—and need the spark of energy and the oil of persistence to develop it. Jim Ryun is a tremendous competitor. But more than that, he is a fine young man—one who did not let discouragement defeat him. He deserves congratulation by adults and emulation by young people.

It was a warming response, but it also carried a hint of the bitter trials that awaited him.

6

Orinpikku Mudo

Excitement mounted as the words FASTEN SEAT BELTS flashed in the front of the cabin. Then the huge jet began its descent through the clouds. Below lay Japan. Young Jim Ryun was thrilled by the prospect of visiting a foreign land. But because he would have to maintain a rigorous training, he had decided that most of his sightseeing would have to wait until after the Olympics. Still, he was consumed by curiosity and excitement on his first day in the Orient.

Impatiently, the United States athletes in their natty red blazers waited aboard their plane until a uniformed Japanese quarantine inspector completed his checkup. Then they walked down the metal steps to the runway. At a nearby hangar, they were herded into three lines. Papers were inspected.

Passports were checked and stamped. Finally the athletes boarded a chartered bus for their trip to the Olympic Village.

They peered eagerly out the windows as the bus sped away from the airport and onto a modern expressway that curved and twisted past the harbor, then cut through bustling downtown Tokyo.

"Look, it's the monorail."

"Get a load of that high building. I didn't think they had any in Japan."

Everything seemed amazingly modern. All along the highway, flags of the competing nations fluttered lightly. White banners, bearing the Olympic red ball and five rings, were draped on store fronts and office buildings along the route. Red and yellow flowers beamed from neat beds on both sides of the road. The face of Tokyo, scrubbed and gleaming, surprised and pleased the Americans. Their bus rolled past the Imperial Palace, the new Olympic judo hall and the Shibuya residential area. As the bus emerged from an underpass, Jim and the others glimpsed dozens of multi-colored flags that marked an access road to Washington Heights and their home for the next month, the Olympic Village.

A guard boarded the bus at the gates of the Village. Yes, this was part of the United States Olympic team. No, there were no impostors on the bus. No, there were no women. Yes, they could enter the Village. *Domo arigato*—thank you very much.

At their yellow barracks, Jim and his two roommates, Oregonians Dyrol Burleson and 30-year-old Bill Dellinger, unpacked their suitcases. In many ways, Jim supposed, this was how it felt to start college. Washington Heights is a former U. S. military housing area, and both Jim's crowded room and the clean but plain barracks atmosphere seemed much as he imagined a college dormitory would be. Outside, however, the atmosphere was different. It was like an international carnival. As soon as the three roommates had unpacked their clothes and arranged their toilet articles on the dresser tops, they set out to explore.

All of Tokyo, the Americans learned, was caught up in the same festive mood as the Village—*orinpikku mudo,* that is, the spirit of the Olympics. The streets in the 165-acre Olympic Village were named after previous Olympic sites—Athens, Rome, Helsinki, Berlin (although the Japanese sign painters had taken a few liberties with the English spellings, arriving at such humorous variations as "Melbourun Street" and "London Stret"). Athletes pedaling bicycles could be seen on almost every street.

The barracks next to the United States team was occupied by the Rumanians. The Russians were quartered in the next building down the line. The Yanks promptly learned to identify them by their blue trousers and brown paisley sport shirts. But the Russian track team was not living in the Village. Instead, their coach had taken his athletes to Nikko, almost two hours away from the distractions of the city.

A warning to frivolous rivals? In front of the Russian barracks, behind a table littered with pamphlets and booklets, sat a studious-looking man offering literature on sports in the Soviet Union to any passers-by who were interested enough to pause and stare.

Athletes of all the nations congregated in the International Club, where milk, tea, Ovaltine and ice cream were free of charge. Next to Australians in their distinctive green blazers, the Americans saw dark-skinned Ghanaians attired in shirts decorated with bright-red flowers, green leaves and a portrait of Ghana's president, Kwame Nkrumah. Along the outskirts of the compound, Japanese boys and girls poked papers, pads and pencils through the wire fences for the athletes to sign. There were autograph hunters even inside the Village. Cleaning women with their tiny brooms and shovels all seemed to have autograph books tucked in the folds of their garments, and all knew enough English to ask, "You sign?"

Police of the Japanese Self-Defense Force snapped away with their cameras and often asked to pose alongside of athletes, especially very tall and very muscular ones. Beds of flowers and neatly clipped hedges bordered the pathways. In the vast, noisy dining hall, which offered such specialties as mutton soup from North Africa and beer soup from Czechoslovakia, as well as Japanese *sukiyaki*, Dellinger made the happy discovery that he could feast on his favorite fruit, bananas.

Stores in the Olympic Village offered cut-rate, tax-free kimonos, sandals, binoculars, cameras, television sets, pearls and other Japanese merchandise. Dellinger, Burleson and Ryun decided that for one day they should give Tokyo its due and try to satisfy some of their curiosity about the great Japanese city of ten-and-a-half million people. After that, they would concentrate on their running.

At the Mitsukoshi department store, Jim saw a 39-foot-tall wooden statue in a glittering, palatial entranceway. The clerks were polite and friendly. There were even uniformed girls standing at the top and bottom of the escalators to help shoppers step on and off the moving stairs. All the subway trains and platforms looked clean and tidy. In the Ginza, an area containing many interesting shops and night-clubs, the lights sparkled red, blue, yellow and white. Jim chuckled at a typical sign outside one little shop: "Talk with you in English, Français and Russian. An opportunity too good for foreign guests."

Orinpikku mudo was evident in all the stores. Other United States athletes strolled the crowded streets in their five-gallon "LBJ" hats. Some carried red and white Olympic shopping bags from another depart-ment store, called Seibu, where a special section dis-played dozens of souvenir items bearing either the Olympic-ring emblem or the legend "Tokyo, 1964." The souvenirs included cuff links, tie clasps, music boxes, scarves, purses, clocks, spoons, cigarette light-ers, *sake* cups, silk neckties, and towels.

"This is fantastic," murmured Jim. Burleson and Dellinger exchanged smiles. Before he finished, Jim bought a movie camera, kimonos for his mother and sister, hand-carved ivory chess sets for himself and his brother, Jerry, as well as a number of ashtrays and other little knickknacks.

Through the busy streets squealed hundreds of brightly painted taxicabs, horns honking incessantly. Apparently each driver made up his own rules as he zipped in and out of traffic. Most of the cabs advertised their rates in bold letters: "100 yen—28 cents, 2 kilometers—$1\frac{1}{4}$ miles." Some were fitted out with maps of Tokyo painted on the plastic seat covers.

At first, it was difficult to get around, but language problems were usually overcome without much fuss. Jim and the other long-legged Americans soon learned a phrase that they found necessary in the stores and along the crowded sidewalks—"*Gomen kudasai*," or "Excuse me."

After their whirlwind introduction to the sights and sounds of Tokyo, Jim and his roommates found some difficulty in adjusting to their new routine. Their problems, after all, were more involved than those of average travelers in a foreign country. Ryun's special problems included an ingrown toenail (which the team trainer had to trim); some sickness from his series of immunizing shots for tetanus, typhoid fever and cholera; and finally, a case of the sniffles which stubbornly refused to go away. Hurriedly, he dashed off notes to his parents and his coach. To Timmons he wrote, "They keep us very busy and I doubt if I can right very often." Timmons doubted it, too, when he noticed the misspelling of the word "write." English had never been Jim's best subject, but still . . .

Both of Jim's roommates caught colds, too. Burleson announced he was taking his virus to bed and staying there until he felt better. However, Dellinger didn't want to sacrifice any workouts. He was training to run the 5,000-meters against Ron Clarke of Australia, Michel Jazy of France, Harald Norpoth of Germany and teammate Bob Schul, holder of the world two-mile record. Instead, Dellinger said he would continue his workouts, trying to snatch extra rest between practices. Ryun decided to do the same. Together, they traveled to practice in sprawling Meiji Park, whose grounds included the National Stadium where the Games would begin in little more than a week.

For three days, Burleson stayed in bed. Ryun and Dellinger spent hours resting, playing blackjack for the little AAU pins that the athletes liked to swap for badges of the other nations. Twice a day, however, Ryun and Dellinger ran and exercised. They saw very little of O'Hara, Uncle Sam's other contender in the 1,500-meters against powerful Peter Snell of New Zealand, Josef Odlozil of Czechoslovakia, Alan Simpson of Britain and Snell's countryman John Davies.

The endless goings and comings of runners and jumpers, weight throwers and wrestlers, swimmers and oarsmen from all over the world served as daily reminders of the great international struggles that lay ahead. Ryun, the 17-year-old "baby" of the United States team, constantly received advice from team-mates. He remembered Timmons' warnings—"Don't try to copy O'Hara's training or anybody else's. Follow your own schedule."

As best he could, he followed it. Sometimes, with his cold and the strangeness of everything, he felt as if he was merely going through the motions. He could only dimly perceive what it might be like to run the 1,500-meters in Tokyo's lavish National Stadium, in front of a crowd of 75,000 and the assembled press of 98 nations.

"At that age, you realize you're going to the Olympics but you really can't understand how tough they are until you see the other athletes," Californian Bob Mathias had warned. Mathias knew. He had been the 17-year-old baby of the United States team at the XIV Olympiad in London in 1948. "It'll be real tough for Ryun," Mathias had added sympathetically.

Mathias didn't realize just how tough. Jim felt so weak and run down from his cold that he decided not to go on a special tour of the Japanese Emperor's palace. Two nights before the opening of the Games, a downpour drenched Tokyo. Jim's throat was sore, his muscles ached and his spirits—along with those of most inhabitants of the Olympic Village—sagged at the sight of thousands of soggy paper and bamboo umbrellas moving along the puddled roadways of the Village. The drizzle continued most of the following morning, but by the eve of the Olympics the skies began to clear. Saturday morning dawned bright and pleasant, a nearly ideal day for the official opening ceremonies.

Thousands of Japanese, many carrying transistor radios, binoculars and cameras, lined the roads to National Stadium. Inside the stadium, 75,778 spectators watched as the dramatic spectacle unfolded. The red, oval running track stood out in vivid contrast to the grassy green center of the mammoth enclosure. Bell-like music signaled the entrance of the emperor and his wife. Then the Japanese national anthem was played. Far below and to the left of the emperor's box, the parade of national teams began, led by the blue-and-white banner of Greece, birthplace of the Olympic Games. The Australian girls, in yellow, then the Bulgarian girls, in red, passed proudly in review. Team by team they circled the track and took their places in the infield—yellow-robed athletes from the Cameroons, pink-clad German girls, turbaned Indians, Americans in their white slacks and red jackets, Russians in their tan suits. Ten thousand balloons soared upward, filling the sky overhead with color. The Olympic flag was raised above the huge electric message board, whose bulbs blinked into words spelling the motto of the Games—*"Citius, altius, fortius."* "Swifter, higher, stronger."

Cameras were forbidden in the parade, but as the

ceremonies went on, men and women of the many Olympic teams could be seen—furtively at first, openly later on—snapping pictures that they would treasure all their lives. At one end of the stadium, a slim Japanese boy came into view, trotting down the track with the flaming Olympic torch in his right hand. A hush fell over the crowd as he circled the track. Then he climbed the 230 carpeted steps and lit a cauldron, which would burn steadily throughout the two weeks of the Olympiad. Together, the athletes recited the Olympic oath: "In the name of all competitors, I promise that we will take part in these Olympic Games, respecting and abiding by the rules which govern them, in the true spirit of sportsmanship, for the glory of sport and the honor of our teams."

Eight thousand doves fluttered into the sky. Five jet planes swooped into sight and traced, in smoke, the Olympic symbol of five interlocking rings—blue, green, white, yellow and pink. The diminutive emperor, only 5 feet 3 inches tall, but highly solemn and dignified in his dark suit and gray tie, bowed and made his exit. While fireworks blazed and crackled, the athletes marched off. The pomp and pageantry were over. It was time for the bitter competition for fame and glory to begin.

7

The Trials of Tokyo

On Sunday, October 11, the gold medals started
to clink. But, of all the sports represented in the 1964
Oympic Games, track and field would be almost the
last to begin. Jim Ryun and his track teammates had
nothing to do but work out and wait impatiently for
Wednesday.

The first gold medal of the Olympics belonged to
Russia—in weight lifting. Soon after came the news
that, in a heat of the single sculls, oarsman Don Spero
of the United States had upset Vyacheslav Ivanov, the
Soviets' proud winner of two previous Olympic gold
medals.

Good signs? Bad signs? For athletes who believed
in omens, there were signs on opening day that the
Olympics would be either glorious or sad or a com-

bination of both. But there was no doubt about one aspect of the Games—they were bound to be used as ammunition in the cold war between the Communist countries and those countries known as the "free world." As Monday wore on, United States supporters exulted over a 100-meter freestyle swimming victory by blond Don Schollander. Then Communists all over the globe welcomed the news of a gold medal won in the women's 200-meter breaststroke by plump, 16-year-old Galina Prozumenschikova. Her last name contained so many letters that all of them wouldn't fit on the electric scoreboard.

In her brief victory speech, the Soviet schoolgirl told the athletes from nations on both sides of the so-called Iron Curtain that their victories would be hailed as more than individual triumphs. That is, they would be offered as proof of a superior way of life (implying that life in Communist countries was better). Then, in a simple but challenging gesture, she dedicated her victory to the crew of her country's newly launched spacecraft, the *Voskhod*.

Yale's Bob Giegengack, head coach of the United States track team, tried to remind his athletes for the last time: "It's not one team against another; it's one individual against another, even your teammates. You're competing to be the best in the world. I'm not even sure that team events like basketball should be in the Olympics. They're not really in the same spirit as track."

On Tuesday night, as threatening clouds drifted

over Tokyo, the coach sensed that his runners and jumpers were on edge. "I don't know whether the athletes are making the coaches nervous or whether we're doing it to them," Giegengack fretted. "But everyone is trying to be nice and kind to everyone else and I think we're ready to snap each other's heads off."

Even easygoing Jim Ryun would have been irritable, except for one thing. He had made an overseas phone call to Wichita during the day. "James, your father and I are coming to Japan," he heard his mother's voice announce happily over the crackling and whirring sounds of the transpacific connection.

"Really? Gee, that's great. I thought it was too expensive."

"Well, it really is. I'll tell you all about it when we get there. But the Kiwanis Club and some other organizations in town took up collections in all the high schools and raised more than $3,000 for our trip. We'll even have a place to stay. The Oriental Missionary Society has a room for us not too far from Tokyo. James, when are you supposed to race?"

"My first trial is on Saturday, Mom. When will you get here?"

"We'll be there Friday, son. We'll be able to see you run."

Jim was overjoyed. That night nothing spoiled his good mood—not even the gathering storm or the discomfort and weakness that resulted from his persistent cold.

That same day a report on the opposition arrived. Tom O'Hara, the frail 1,500-meter runner from Loyola of Chicago, ran a half-mile workout against muscular, 176-pound Peter Snell of New Zealand. Snell, 26 years old, was the defending champion in the 800-meters and the favorite at both 800 and 1,500-meters. The piston-legged Snell had pulled away from O'Hara so powerfully at the finish that it wasn't even a contest.

"Wow, is he tough!" muttered O'Hara. "He's so strong. So strong."

There was one more bit of bad news. In his last practice workout, little Gerry Lindgren, top hope of the United States in Wednesday's 10,000-meters (six miles, 376 yards), stepped in a hole and turned his ankle. Then, instead of getting prompt treatment, the inexperienced 18-year-old runner waited three hours before going to the team trainer. By Tuesday night, he was limping badly on a puffy leg.

Wednesday was stormy. By noon, the red brick-dust track had been darkened by the rain and pocked with puddles. Then the temperature dropped into the low 60s and the rain slackened. About fifteen minutes before the call for the 10,000-meters, a weak sun slanted into the stadium. Early in the race it became painfully obvious to the Americans that Lindgren was not going to win. He was in too much pain, running too stiffly. Not until late in the race did Lindgren's cheering teammates on the sidelines realize that another blue-jerseyed American, Billy Mills, had a very real chance for victory. Mills set a fast early pace and kept it up until reporters in the press box, convinced he had enough stamina and determination to stay in contention, began to leaf through their files on the United States athletes. Billy Mills? Who was Billy Mills?

Ryun knew Mills, mostly because they were both Kansas boys. Billy Mills was part Sioux Indian, educated at the Haskell Indian Institute and then at the University of Kansas, both in Lawrence. Few others, however, had ever heard of him. Not a single newspaper or magazine writer had talked to him in all the time he had been in Tokyo.

On the 25th and last quarter-mile lap, Mills sprinted from ten yards back, passed the favored Ron Clarke of Australia and two other rivals, and plunged across the finish line wearing an unforgettable expression of mingled pain and pride. Mills had set an Olympic record of 28 minutes, 24.4 seconds in a race no one had dreamed he might win.

There was sadness, too, in the finish of the 10,000-meters. Almost a full minute after Mills crossed the line, waiflike Gerry Lindgren limped in, a forlorn ninth. Alone and unhappy, Lindgren walked slowly out of the stadium and thirstily gulped a cup of chocolate drink at a deserted snack stand.

More rain was expected on Thursday, but the clouds vanished, leaving blue skies and warm sunshine for a day that proved memorable to Mills's inspired teammates. Big-armed discus thrower Al Oerter of West Babylon, New York, strapped up like a mummy after having torn muscle fibers and a cartilage in his side in practice five days earlier, unleashed a final toss of 200 feet, 1½ inches to take the gold medal from favored Ludvik Danek of Czechoslovakia. In the single-sculls final, Don Spero was beaten by Ivanov and five others, but the Vesper Boat Club of Philadelphia won first place in the eight-oared crew final. Don Schollander thrashed to another gold medal. Other United States athletes added five more first places in swimming, diving, rowing, rifle and track. The last of the five was won by broad-chested sprinter Bob Hayes of Jacksonville, Florida, who galloped over a chewed-up section of the track to win the 100-meters.

"Tonight," said the 21-year-old Hayes, beaming, "I'm going to take my mother out and show her the town."

On Friday, the day Jim Ryun's parents reached Tokyo, still another injured American set a courageous example for his teammates. Most of them knew that hurdler Warren "Rex" Cawley had hurt his thigh before the team left California, then hurt it again in a Tokyo workout. Although he was so nervous that he could hardly doff his warm-up togs, the 24-year-old Cawley managed to turn off both his nerves and the pain. He sped over the 400-meter course to win the race for the United States.

It was also a day of triumph for Ryun's roommate Bill Dellinger, who qualified for the 5,000-meter

New Zealand's Peter Snell wins the 800-meter final. He was favored to win the 1,500-meter, too.

final. On the same day, New Zealand's formidable Peter Snell blazed to victory in the 800-meter final. That was one gold medal for Snell, and most observers expected him to win one more.

"The pressure was terrific," remarked Snell, sounding a little less sure of himself than usual. "I'll try to qualify in the 1,500 tomorrow, but it will be most difficult without a day off."

It was difficult enough for Jim Ryun even without the added burden of an earlier race. Snell simply frightened him. Jim was glad to find that Dyrol Bur-

leson was running in Saturday's first heat. Jim himself
was scheduled for the second heat and Snell was
listed in the third, along with Tom O'Hara. In all,
there were four heats. The first four finishers in each
nine-man heat would qualify for Monday's semifinals, which in turn would narrow the field to nine for
Wednesday's final.

Burleson survived the first heat, placing third. The
elbowing and jostling looked fearsome to Jim, who
made up his mind to stay clear of the mob and any
possible traps, even if running along the outside of

*During his qualifying heat, Jim ran on the outside of the pack and
placed fourth.*

the pack meant he had to travel many yards farther than his opponents. He knew practically nothing about his nine rivals in the heat. All he knew was that he had to run faster than six of them, which is exactly what he did. His time of 3:44.4. was just good enough to place him fourth—behind Michael Bernard of France, Jürgen May of Germany and John Whetton of Great Britain—and squeeze him into the semifinals.

Jim won praise from Coach Giegengack for running in the outside lane. "Good strategy," Giegengack complimented him. "In a race like that, it's a good idea to stay out of trouble." Even though Jim's course had forced him to add as much as 40 meters to the total distance, he still ran his heat faster than Burleson, O'Hara and Snell had run theirs. Snell, the favorite, coasted in fourth in his race, unconcerned over finishing behind O'Hara and two others. He ran no harder than he had to.

Jim felt good, although he wasn't really as confident as he seemed in the postcard he dispatched that evening to Bob Timmons, back in the United States:

Dear Bob,

Well, I made it through the preliminaries and am on my way to a Gold Medal. I'm sorry about not calling, but the cables to the U. S. are bad and no one could get through. I'm still trying but am getting nowhere. I will call as soon as possible.

Sincerely,
Jim Ryun

Jim's knee, injured in a fall earlier in the season, ached badly on Sunday. It was another rainy day, and his cold felt worse. His parents went to morning services at the Church of Christ, but Jim stayed in bed most of the morning, resting. At lunch in the Olympic Village, his mother noticed how jittery he seemed. She tried to comfort him, but didn't have much success.

"I wish Timmie was here," Jim admitted.

That afternoon, Bob Schul of Ohio scored a magnificent upset victory in the 5,000-meters. Jim's roommate Dellinger earned a bronze medal by placing third. Schul crowed, "They've been telling us for years that we Americans are softies and couldn't win anything but the sprints. I guess we showed the world we could do it."

To complete their sense of victory the Yanks had only to win the 1,500-meters—an event no United States runner had won since Melvin W. Sheppard in 1908. Could it be done, competing against the great Snell?

On the morning of the 1,500-meter semifinal, Jim didn't see his parents at all. Before the runners took their marks, coach Giegengack warned, "Don't figure on saving anything for the next race or there may not be a next race. I want you to run this heat just like it's the final. As far as I'm concerned, you're going for the gold medal."

Peter Snell ran that way. Ryun, the only American in the first heat, wished he had been paired with

Burleson or even O'Hara instead of being forced to run against Snell. His strategy had little to do with Snell, just the same. He would avoid Snell and all the rest, stay in the outside lane and run his own race. It was an easy tactic to follow, but this time it failed.

With two laps to go, Snell and most of his pursuers stepped up their pace. Suddenly, to his dismay, Jim discovered that strategy didn't matter. Nor did all his determination. All that mattered was the full, clear, cruel knowledge that he was steadily, helplessly falling back in the race in which he could least afford to lag, the one he wanted most to win. Jim's throat was dry. Pain shot through his muscles, from his breastbone all the way down to his calves. Worst of all, his legs refused to obey his frantic commands. As Snell swept powerfully into the final turn and drove forward to the wire, Ryun struggled in pain and shame, forcing himself to complete the race, although he was 150 yards behind Snell. His position was one he couldn't remember enduring since junior high school—last place.

Uncomprehending, like a boy having a nightmare, Jim heard his time. It was 3:55 , fully 11 seconds slower than his qualifying time three days earlier and 16 seconds slower than his best clocking for the metric mile. Numb, he haltingly answered the reporters' questions.

"The pressure? No, that didn't get me. I felt more relaxed today than in my preliminary heat. No, I really don't know what went wrong, I felt good before the race. I didn't expect the pace to be that fast, but the coach warned us about that. No, I just don't have any excuses."

Jim did have excuses, of course. Legitimate excuses. He just couldn't bring himself to mention them. His poor health was undeniably the main reason for his last-place showing. But the cold that had kept him in bed at least part of every day for two weeks seemed such a flimsy reason for failure. Other runners had colds, after all. Bill Dellinger had one. Dyrol Burleson had one. Jim felt that it was his own fault for not taking better care of himself and recovering from the cold in time. He answered the questions patiently, trying not to show how near to tears he felt. Finally the ordeal was over, and he listened to words of consolation from his mother—who had been permitted to come onto the field by a sympathetic guard —and, later, from Burleson and his wife. What could anyone say? How could anyone really understand?

Heartsick and still dazed, Jim watched Burleson win the second 1,500-meter heat in 3:41.5, about three seconds slower than Snell's clocking. O'Hara finished 7th and also failed to qualify for the final.

So Jim Ryun's role in the Olympics was ended. He packed his sweat clothes and track shoes, his shirts and ties and souvenirs, and moved out of the Olympic Village barracks to join his parents in the missionary compound. Together, the three of them browsed in curio shops, visited shrines and, moving eagerly from distraction to distraction, assumed the role of American tourists in Japan. Jim didn't want to think about track.

The news of Peter Snell's victory in the 1,500-meter final neither surprised nor moved him. Mostly, Jim felt sorry for Burleson, who had worked so hard and sacrificed so much to succeed, only to find himself boxed in on the last lap like a beginner, and hardly able to escape in time to finish fifth. Burley was a good loser, though. Jim learned a lot about grace and courage just from watching him.

Mostly from habit, Jim arose early each day at the missionary compound and ran his customary five or six miles on the dusty roads outside of town. He didn't enjoy it. It was simply something to do, something he felt he had to do.

Late in the week, Jim received a letter from Bob Timmons. Like Burleson, Dellinger and Jim's parents, Timmie tried to soften the sting of defeat by talking about the future. Jim read the letter several times. It said, in part:

Nobody can stay at a fever pitch level and compete week in and week out and perform at his best. This is normal in competition and it is something that each of us must accept. If this were not the case, then everyone would be a winner all the time and all the sparkle, enthusiasm and thrill of competition would be tarnished by a monotonous winning. . . .

"Monotonous winning," reflected Jim. In a sense, it

was true. But oh, how much of that monotonous winning he would happily trade for a gold medal in the Olympic Games! And now his chance was gone.

Timmons' letter continued:

. . . I suggest you look back on your experience in Tokyo as one of learning. Benefit from studying through your errors and miscalculations, if there were any, and determine how you might have eliminated them if you had them to do again. Think about your mental preparation, your training program, your tactical plans, the overall situation of those of your opponents . . . Select from them the things that will make you a better runner in the future.

There is no doubt in my mind that you will become the greatest middle-distance runner in the history of the world . . . Just remember, Jim, it was just two years ago that you ran 5:38 on the mile and now you have gone all the way down to the equivalent of a 3:56 flat. This is probably the most phenomenal story in the history of distance running. You can extend it way down below the 3:50 level . . .

"Good old Timmie," thought Jim. "There he goes again." Yet everything the coach had promised so far had come true. Through pain and persistence, Jim had accomplished more than he or anyone else thought possible. Was it really worth the effort, though? Was it worth going on to more pain, more monotony, more winning—and more heartbreak? Jim honestly didn't know.

The closing ceremonies of the 1964 Olympics.

On the day of closing ceremonies in National Stadium, Jim's parents left early to catch a California-bound jet. The United States athletes, led by swimmer Don Schollander—winner of four gold medals—marched proudly around the track. Altogether, the Americans had won 36 gold medals. The Russians, who had kept such a careful box score at the Rome Olympics in 1960, were not talking about team totals any more. They had won only 30 gold medals. In men's track, the Yanks won as many gold medals (12) as the rest of the competing countries together. Although Jim Ryun considered his own effort a subject of shame and chagrin, he could not help feeling a surge of pride in the accomplishments of America's athletes.

As the stadium lights dimmed, 200 women gymnasts carrying torches formed a huge circle around the assembled athletes. The band played the national anthem of Japan, followed by the national anthem of Mexico, the host to the next Olympics. The voice of Avery Brundage of the United States, chairman of the International Olympic Committee, boomed from the loudspeakers: "I declare the Games of the Eighteenth Olympiad closed, and in accordance with tradition, I call upon the youth of all countries to assemble four years from now . . . at Mexico City."

Now the only light remaining in the vast stadium was a single, gleaming spotlight focused on the Olympic flag. The flag was slowly lowered, carried past the box of the Emperor of Japan, then out of the stadium gates. The band struck up "Auld Lang Syne." The Japanese word for farewell, *"Sayonara,"* appeared in white lights on the huge message board. Thousands of white handkerchiefs fluttered in the grandstand, and in a final burst of color, fireworks showered the sky over Tokyo.

To 17-year-old Jim Ryun, about to begin his senior year in high school, the Mexico City Olympics of 1968 seemed far away. First, he had to discover anew the qualities that Timmons had touched on in his letter—the sparkle, enthusiasm and thrill of competition. Then, and only then, could Jim hope to make the coach's latest prediction come true.

8

Making a Friend of Peter

As he struggled clumsily with his suitcases in the midst of a welcoming committee that was shuffling slowly toward the waiting room of the Wichita Municipal Airport, Jim wished the public, even the open-armed, warm-hearted public, might some day decide to ignore him completely.

Did they think he was proud of himself, coming home, after two and a half months, as a loser in the Olympics? Would they think he was showing off, just because of the five-gallon hat on his head? The hat was so easily explained, really. There was no room for it in his stuffed suitcases and duffle bags. He knew he worried too much about little things like that, but these receptions always embarrassed him. It was comforting to know that he was coming back as the captain of the East High cross-country team, although it had completed all but two of its meets.

After his first night at home, Jim found himself too busy to devote much thought to the Olympics. The Class AA regional cross-country meet was scheduled for the very next weekend. And the schoolwork, whew! There was so much to make up!

Jim had tried conscientiously to keep up with his textbook reading in Tokyo—especially in English, which he found difficult. But in mechanical drawing alone, there were so many drafting plates to be sketched that almost every night he found himself nodding sleepily over the drawing board in his basement room. He stayed up late so often, in fact, that by the time Christmas vacation arrived, he decided to give up his morning running for a while. It was the only way he could get the drawings done on time.

Jim's fears over cross-country were unfounded, of course. He won both the regional and state meets. All the schoolwork made the time pass fast. Once the first semester was over, and his classwork was straightened out, Jim again found himself looking forward eagerly to the challenge of the outdoor track season.

His new coach at East High, J. D. Edmiston, undoubtedly helped to bolster Jim's state of mind a great deal. Edmiston's boys knew that there was one thing J. D. couldn't stand—monotony. Unlike Timmie, who sometimes seemed to behave like a slave driver, J. D. was easygoing. He would saunter up to his sweating athletes, a pencil tucked behind

Edmiston treated Ryun more as an equal than as a pupil.

his right ear, and crack a joke, make a face or say something to lighten the drudgery.

"You think you're fooling me, huh?" J. D. would ask with a wink. "Naw, you're not. Every time you jake it, every time you take it easy on yourself, you think you're cheating me? You're just cheating your teammates—and fooling yourself. Don't get me wrong. I think track should be fun. If you're not having any fun, forget it. But the most fun of all is winning. It always will be."

Edmiston used a different approach with Ryun, though. Winning against high-school competition came easily to Jim by this time, and the husky, wise-cracking coach tried to keep Ryun happy by treating him more as an equal than as a pupil. J. D. recognized the strength of Ryun's inner drives. He also knew that Jim's tremendous individual motivation was accompanied by an equally strong team spirit. Fellow runners realized this, too. They knew Ryun was capable of more work and needed more work than the rest of the team. As a result, he also contributed more. It was enough for them to try to follow his example.

Some, like fun-loving Mike Petterson, soon discovered that trying to keep up with Jim in practice every day made them faster, stronger runners. Ryun, Petterson and three others made up Edmiston's special distance group, an elite corps which earned special privileges because all five of the boys had proved their willingness to work harder in order to improve.

The better he got to know J. D., the more Jim liked him. But he also kept in touch with Timmons at the University of Kansas. In March, 1965, Timmons accepted an offer to become the new head coach of track at Oregon State. It seemed perfectly natural to Jim that he, too, should plan to enter Oregon State.

Jim and teammate Mike Petterson pose on the winners' stand during the Kansas State High-School Championships in May, 1965.

Dyrol Burleson and Bill Dellinger had convinced him that Oregon was a fine state in which to live. Now, with Timmie going there, too . . .

Thinking about his relationship with his former coach, Jim felt that Timmie didn't always understand him any more. Sometimes, perhaps, he treated Jim more like a child than the fast-maturing teen-ager could stand. But basically, they understood each other. There was that night when Timmie had insisted that Ryun run both the mile and half-mile in the Missouri Valley AAU meet, and Jim had said he couldn't do it, and yet . . . Yes, he owed Timmie a lot.

Until April, Jim didn't realize the strength of his debt. Then, abruptly, Bill Easton, the head track coach at the University of Kansas, was fired. The job was offered to Timmons, who had been Easton's assistant. After confirming that his former boss had no chance of keeping the job, Timmons decided to change his plans and accept it.

Jim thought quite seriously about this new development. At length, he decided to change his own plans and follow Timmie to KU. He wrote a polite letter to Oregon State, turning down its offer of a track scholarship. Then he accepted KU's nearly identical scholarship offer—free room, board and tuition. Of course, Timmons was delighted. So were Mr. and Mrs. Ryun, Jim's schoolmates and the local reporters who had followed his high-school athletic career so avidly.

That spring, Jim's high-school races amounted to nothing more than competitions against the clock. That was incentive enough, however. Jim was preparing for the June invitational meets in California, where the opposition would come from such runners as New Zealander Peter Snell and Czech Josef Odlozil, winners of Olympic gold and silver medals in the 1,500-meters.

Because Jim was so much faster than his high-school opponents, he had to concentrate on the stopwatch in order to keep improving. Running against time required him to perfect his sense of pace. After he and J. D. set up the goal for each race, they would work out a series of "splits," or times for each 220 yards, just as Jim had done earlier with Timmons. Hearing his time halfway around each quarter-mile lap, Jim would know if his pace had begun to lag and could strive immediately to speed it up.

In Jim's final high-school mile, at the Wichita State University stadium, he not only won the state title again, but dashed home in 3:58.3 for the fastest mile of the year in the United States. Congressman Garner Shriver of Kansas stood up on the floor of the House of Representatives in Washington, D. C., and asked that the feat be inscribed in the Congressional Record. The Congressman pointed out that Jim Ryun of Wichita had again run the fastest mile to be achieved by a high-school boy.

Two weeks later, at a meet in Modesto, California, Jim's chief rival in the mile event was college graduate Jim Grelle. Ryun lost the lead early on the final lap, after racing shoulder to shoulder with Grelle, but finally sprinted to victory in 3 minutes, 58.1 seconds. He returned to Kansas from California on Sunday for his high-school graduation the following night.

At commencement exercises in East High, Jim was startled to hear loud applause following the announcement of his name. He smiled self-consciously as he walked up to receive his diploma. The hand-clapping continued. Jim's face turned a deep red. Every person in the auditorium was standing up, paying him tribute.

Jim didn't go to the Senior Prom. He never went to dances, so he didn't feel bad about missing this one. His mind was on the mile event in the Compton Relays in California. For the first time, the Relays were not going to be run at Compton. Instead, the meet was being moved to the Los Angeles Coliseum to take advantage of its immense spectator facilities. One reason why more room was needed for spectators was that the world's champion miler, New Zealand's Peter Snell, would be there.

Jim was nervous over the prospect of competing against Snell again. During the tense trip to Los Angeles, Edmiston jokingly said to him, "I don't see how you can eat so much," after watching him devour a full meal on the Wichita-to-Denver leg of their flight, then put away a huge dessert in the airport restaurant at Denver.

At the starting line Ryun watches Snell closely.

"I have cavities in both legs," quipped Jim, trying to smile.

However, his attempt to wisecrack and J. D.'s lightheartedness were not enough to relieve Ryun's jitters. On the night of the race, Jim's fingers shook as he pinned number 114 to his jersey. It looked crooked, but he felt too ill at ease to try pinning it on straight. Out under the floodlights of the huge Coliseum, the feeling of immaturity that gripped him was in sharp contrast to his feeling of importance at graduation only a short time before. As he warmed up, he looked over the huge crowd, trying to find

Edmiston. No luck. Jim would have liked to walk down the track to look for him, but he hated to parade in front of all those people.

As Snell warmed up, Jim watched him in awe. He tried to concentrate on his own preparations, but his eyes kept darting back to Snell. At the starting line, he studied Snell in wide-eyed fascination. Regrettably, Jim wasn't able to watch Snell long enough. A few moments later, the race began.

When the gun barked, signaling the start of the last lap, Jim heard his own time—3:01 and a fraction—and realized that in spite of the extra-fast pace, he still felt strong. He geared himself mentally for the finishing sprint, wondering how strong Snell might feel going into the last half-lap.

Snell was strong, all right. And shrewd. Instead of waiting for the last 220 yards to launch his kick, the New Zealander started it as soon as he rounded the turn into the backstretch. Too late, Jim realized that Snell had fooled him and the others. Already trailing by nearly ten yards, Jim started his own sprint. He knew his only chance of winning hung on the faint hope that Snell might waver. It was no use. Snell won and even Jim Grelle nosed Jim out for second place, although Ryun had the satisfaction of running 3:56.8, his fastest mile.

After Jim's warmdown, he tried to congratulate Snell, but couldn't get close enough to the popular champion to shake his hand. Jim went into the locker room, took a shower and dressed. Again he tried to

Ryun waits patiently to congratulate Snell.

approach Snell. Shyly, Jim attempted to press through the small ring of autograph hunters and well-wishers that still surrounded Snell. Once, he thought he caught Snell's eye and quickly thrust out his hand. No, Snell didn't seem to notice. Instead, the New Zealander turned away and began to talk to a stranger in a baseball cap.

Feeling that he was being snubbed, but determined now to finish what he had started, Jim waited until every person in the group had spoken to Snell and moved off. As Snell waved his final good-by, Jim strode forward again and blurted awkwardly, "Nice race, Peter. Congratulations."

Snell looked at him for the first time, muttered, "Thank you," and slipped quickly away to his dressing room.

As he rejoined his coach, Jim sighed, "Boy, I'm glad that's over."

J. D. looked at him intently and said, "Well . . . you can take him next time."

"Yeah, I guess I can," replied the boy. He said it casually, but the coach knew he was serious. He also knew how much it meant to Jim to beat Peter Snell in that next race.

On the way back to the hotel, they discussed it. Jim's next mile against Snell would take place in the AAU championships at San Diego on the last week-end of June, only three weeks away. Ryun must try to run on the inside of the track, instead of running so wide that he had to cover as much as 20 yards more than his rivals over the full mile distance. And he must make his final move earlier—and sustain that sprint speed all the way to the tape.

In the meantime, Jim settled into a daily routine that began with a morning workout at six o'clock, a full day of errands, darkroom and messenger work at the Edwards Typographic Service. The day ended with another long workout at 5:30 P.M. Prior to the

AAU championships, Jim doubled in the Golden West Invitational at Sacramento, California, taking the two-mile in 9:04 and the mile in an almost effortless 4:04.3. Then he won a three-mile all-comers race at Roosevelt Field.

Jim, 18 years old now, had reached the point where he realized that he sometimes disappointed the spectators by failing to break four minutes flat for the mile. It was an unfair twist of fate, but one that Jim was forced to recognize. There were more important considerations than the spectators. The first was Jim's desire to beat Snell. The second was making the United States team that would travel to Russia and Poland later in the summer to oppose the Soviet and Polish national teams.

"The only way to do it is to move before Snell does," Edmiston reminded Jim as they stood together alongside the East High track before the last series of workouts for the San Diego meet. All that week Jim worked on sprints. He would circle the track, pound down the backstretch with his eyes fixed on the brick wall of the field house straight ahead, then shift into high gear for the last 300 yards, charging at full speed as he came abreast of the last light pole before the final curve. After that, it was an all-out effort the rest of the way.

When the night arrived for Jim's first race on the new $20,000 asphalt composition track at San Diego's Balboa Stadium, he and Snell drew starting positions in the same heat of the mile. Jim knew he was physically ready. There could be no excuses on that score. And Edmiston was confident that, mentally, the boy had never been better prepared. Jim thought he could win; he had practiced his gallop for the last 300 yards so many times that the upcoming race seemed to him like a play in which he had fully memorized his role. Still, one small part of him feared that he might forget.

Jim's main purpose in the heat was to qualify for the final. On the last lap, he moved out strongly next to Snell, matched him stride for stride into the stretch and finished the race alongside him. The judges ruled it a dead heat.

Jim, panting heavily, looked up to see Snell approaching.

"Nice race, Jim," puffed the champion. "How do you feel?"

"Just great," replied Jim, stiffening his face muscles and straining to hide his fatigue. "That last quarter couldn't have been faster than 60 seconds."

Later Jim described the brief conversation to Edmiston. Grinning, J. D. nodded happily. He was sure that Jim's air of confidence had left Snell more than a trifle concerned.

J. D. had decided that there was no sense in getting up early the next morning, or staying up, for that matter. So Jim got up, went to church, ate breakfast at 10:45 A.M., then returned to his room and went to bed again. A little after 2:00 P.M. he got up and dressed, ate a steak in the motel coffee shop, and promptly lay down again to rest. He and J. D. drove to the stadium as late as possible.

The mile final followed a stirring six-mile race in which Billy Mills edged Gerry Lindgren at the tape, and both were credited with world-record clockings of 27:11.6. The highly stimulated crowd was eager and excited as the milers jogged onto the track and took their places at the starting line.

With the crack of the gun, both the spectators and the runners sensed something electric. The pace was swift, but none of the eight runners lagged. All remained in a tight little knot through the first lap, then the second. As they approached the start-and-finish line for the next to last time, the starter raised his pistol for the "gun lap" warning and a loud buzz arose in the grandstand. Would all eight milers run the last lap as strongly as they had run the first three? Who would be the first to start a sprint? How long would Snell wait? What about Grelle? And what about Ryun?

Ryun concentrated on Snell. This time, however, the New Zealander waited, counting on his mighty finishing surge. Instead it was the Czech, Odlozil, who burst impatiently out of the pack and swiftly opened a 15-yard gap. Ryun sensed that Odlozil's unexpected sprint might provoke Snell into launching a last effort of him own. Jim could wait no longer. He was too close to the last 300 yards. As planned, he swung out and ran as hard as he could, passed Odlozil and plunged into the final curve, determined to main-

Ryun's pain is apparent as he hits the tape a yard ahead of Snell.

tain that flat-out speed until he either breasted the
tape or keeled over on the track. For an instant,
Grelle and Snell lost sight of Ryun. By the time they
realized how hard he was sprinting, it was too late.
At the end, Ryun was still a yard ahead of Snell and
three yards ahead of Grelle. The winning time was
3:55.3, an American record.

Tired to the point of near sickness, Jim lurched off
the track. Almost immediately, he felt an arm around

Ryun, victorious but humble, poses on the winners' stand alongside Snell.

his neck. Jim looked up to see Snell, the hero he had worshipped, beaming in honest admiration. Jim felt too worn out to respond with anything more than a weak smile and a handclasp. Then he staggered dizzily into the infield, pursued by reporters and several men from a TV network who paid no attention when Jim wearily tried to wave them off. Several times a television technician tried to persuade him to stand in front of a camera near the finish line.

"This is for national TV," he said. "We just want a few words, that's all. It's coast-to-coast."

Jim wasn't impressed. He didn't mean to be rude, but he needed more time to recover. He could barely stand up straight. The technician blocked Jim's path again.

"Okay, okay," groaned Ryun, making a sour face, "But this may be the first nationwide telecast of a runner getting sick to his stomach."

The cameraman hastily retreated out of Jim's range. Later, when he felt sufficiently clear-headed to think about the incident, Jim was quite amused. In many ways, it had been an educational evening.

Afterwards, Jim commented on the race: "This is the first time I had a race strategy and everything worked just like we hoped."

Later that night, as Ryun and the exuberant Edmiston started back to their motel, Jim said softly, "You know, I think I've made a friend out of Peter." Perhaps he had. Certainly he had made a believer.

A few days later, filling out a routine form for the athletic department at Kansas University, Jim listed his two greatest thrills. One was making the United States Olympic team. The other was beating Peter Snell. Once-in-a-lifetime accomplishments? Jim had no way of knowing. All he knew was that he felt as good about running now as he ever had. He was ready—and proud—to go overseas again as a representative of the United States. He was ready to run against the Russians.

9

How Many
Kids Go to Kiev?

Somehow, Jim Ryun was overlooked when the AAU drew up a list of American track stars to send to Europe for a series of meets preceding the United States-Russia and United States-Poland meets. It was obvious that the AAU hadn't expected Ryun to whip Snell, the world's best miler. As a consolation trip, they decided to send Ryun to a three-day meet in Jamaica—a pleasant little island in the West Indies, but scarcely the place Jim would have picked if he had been given his choice. Edmiston wouldn't have picked it either. He was boiling mad.

Jim wasn't nearly as disturbed by the slight, however. At least the state of Kansas wasn't overlooking its native son. Channel 10 in Wichita televised a 30-minute special on Jim. Three days after that, he was voted "Kansas Athlete of the Year." Finally, Wichita arranged a "Jim Ryun Day" in his honor, scheduling a big track meet that was to feature many members of the United States national team, as well as the young hometown hero.

Getting ready for the Jamaica meet, Jim ran his five miles each morning, then put on blue jeans and sport shirt and went to work at the Edwards Typographic Service. His boss, Mr. Waldo Leisy, willingly gave him time off for the trip. In the West Indies, Jim won a mile race and a half-mile race, but lost at three miles. Soon after returning, he noticed a painful stiffness in his right knee. Since he had a bruise on his left foot, Jim suspected that he had wrenched the knee by favoring the sore foot. He was worried about the effect his injured knee would have on the next race.

As Jim Ryun Day approached, Jim began to realize that the Wichita newspapers and television stations expected him to try for a world record in the mile. He was alarmed. The news media could say anything they wanted about the record—he didn't care—but people were buying tickets to the meet, expecting to see him at his best. And he knew he wouldn't be. Unhappily, Jim discussed the problem with Edmiston.

"If running in this meet makes your knee worse," the coach told him firmly, "then you shouldn't run at all. The most important thing is to be ready for that race in Russia."

Jim nodded. The only thing to do, he decided, was to announce that his leg was sore and that he didn't expect to try for a record in the meet. He would be happy just to win.

After work one afternoon, he drove his green Plymouth to television station KTVH. He tried to explain his problem to the station's sports director. As he talked, Jim realized that it was hopeless. He shouldn't run at all, and if it were any other meet, he would simply skip it. But, in order to help lagging ticket sales, he agreed to run.

After losing on "Jim Ryun Day," Jim lies on a training table with an ice pack on his injured knee, while Edmiston unlaces his shoes. Ryun's father is waiting anxiously in the background at the right.

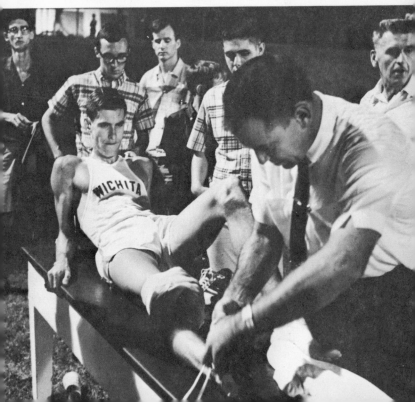

On Thursday, the day before the meet, Jim's doctor injected cortisone into the injured knee. Jim Ryun Day dawned warm and clear, and the temperature soared into the 90s. Jim's knee ached, but he ran. The crowd of 6,600 cheered proudly, even though Jim finished 40 yards behind Morgan Groth, the winner, and the unhappy Wichita lad didn't even break 4:10. As soon as the race was over, an ice pack was slapped on Jim's knee. The next day, it still hurt.

Jim and Edmiston decided to see the coach of the United States team, Brutus Hamilton, who was in town for the meet.

"My knee is pretty bad, Mr. Hamilton," the boy blurted. "I may not be able to run very well in Russia. Maybe I should stay home and let somebody else make the trip."

The coach disagreed. "We don't leave for four days yet," he said. "The meet is a whole week off. You might be just fine by that time. If not, well, I want you to come along anyway. Let's hope for the best."

Although Hamilton talked optimistically to Jim, he had private doubts. Ryun had earned the trip and he was going to make it, but how would the boy perform after a week of little or no practice?

"You can't completely stop a boy like that," Hamilton told a newsman. "All I can do is suggest he go on a light training schedule, with no chance of straining his knee. But Jim is used to hard workouts. What he needs is to rest the knee and probably that sore foot, too. After another week of light work—or no work—

I'm not sure he can be ready even if the leg should be all right."

When Jim arrived in New York City on Monday, he felt better. Busy with all the arrangements for the trip, he almost forgot about his knee. First, the American athletes flew from New York to London, where their plane picked up a Russian pilot. Then they took off for the Soviet Union.

Jim went up to the cockpit and stood in fascination amid the hundreds of dials and control levers. Jim's father worked for Boeing Aircraft. His brother, Jerry, worked for Cessna Aircraft, and Jerry's wife worked for Beech Aircraft. Yet, until Jim stood in front of the massive controls of the Moscow-bound jet, he had never fully appreciated the complexity of a modern airship.

In Moscow, the confusion over passports, luggage and loading was even worse than it had been in Tokyo. Some of the American athletes who had been appearing in other European meets greeted the new arrivals in Moscow. Before enplaning for Kiev, Jim and his companions spent some time sightseeing. Jim bought a big fur hat and several small souvenirs in a department store. He bought a cup and saucer for his mother, something he always tried to do in each city he visited. In Red Square, Muscovites in their bulky suits and dresses stared at the Americans. The Americans stared back. Several of the Russians offered to exchange their coats for the natty blazers worn by the Americans. Jim could see that the curious Muscovites were aware that he and his fellow athletes were from the United States, but they appeared to have no idea that the Americans were there to run against the Russian track team.

By the time the Yanks returned to the airport, reloaded their luggage and finally took off for Kiev, Jim and many of the others were so weary that their nerves were jumping. None of the athletes had slept more than two or three hours since leaving the States. Those who could sleep on the plane caught naps. Jim developed an earache that kept him awake. The landing in Kiev, the drive to the hotel and the scramble to check into his room left him exhausted.

The hotel was a splendid-looking building, fourteen stories high. But the Americans had to wait on the front steps almost two hours while various clerks kept reassuring them that their rooms were being prepared. After a dinner of fish and soda water, Jim fell into bed and slept heavily. The next day, he sent picture post cards to his parents, Edmiston, and Timmons. "We finally made it to Kiev," he wrote, "after 21 hours of confusion and two hours' sleep."

Jim's schedule in Kiev was busier than it had ever been at home. He worked out twice a day, shopped and saw the sights. Everywhere he traveled, he took pictures. Photo editor Rich Clarkson of the Topeka *Capital-Journal* had asked him to send back notes with his impressions of the Soviet Union and its people. Clarkson had suggested that Jim send back snapshots, too.

The newspaper couldn't pay Jim for the articles and photos, of course. According to the strict rules of the AAU, Jim's athletic career had provided the opportunity for the trip, so accepting money as a result of the trip would make him a professional. The newspaper provided the camera and the color film, however, and Jim enjoyed his role as a photographer. He was quite competent, too. In fact, the quality of his pictures was so good that Clarkson used a number of the photos Jim sent home and later gave Jim a job as a part-time staff photographer on the *Capital-Journal*.

After his first few practices, Jim's knee felt better. Between workouts, he happily resumed the role of a wide-eyed American tourist. One of his dispatches to the *Capital-Journal* noted: "Everything in Russia is about what we had in the United States at the turn of the century. Clothes here are high—shirts at $7 and $8 and children's coats at $38 to $45 and of poor quality."

Just before the two-day track meet between the two nations was to begin, Jim sent another dispatch, which predicted, "If we lose the meet, it will be only because some of our athletes are not up to par because of sickness or injury." Jim didn't add that his own condition was far from good. A drug called DMSO made it possible for him to run without too much pain, but his leg remained stiff and sore.

Russia's two 1,500-meter runners, Ivan Belitzky and young Oleg Raiko, greeted Jim and Jim Grelle

Grelle crosses the finish line in 3:39.2 for the fastest 1,500-meter clocking in the U.S.–U.S.S.R. series of meets. Ryun finished second in 3:40.4.

warmly. Grelle reminded Ryun, however, that the Soviets were undoubtedly planning a hot race.

"I think they'll go out hard," surmised Grelle. "If they do, let's try to run our own race, stick to a good, sensible pace and just not let them get too far ahead. Don't let them fool us into burning ourselves out early."

Grelle's guess proved to be a good one. Belitzky and Raiko took off at a torrid clip. Undismayed, the Americans stayed close together, maintaining a strong, steady pace. Late in the race, Grelle and Ryun swept smoothly past the fading Russians. Grelle made a strong sprint and won in 3:39.2, the fastest 1,500-meter clocking of the U.S.-U.S.S.R. series.

Ryun finished second in 3:40.4. Belitzky was timed in 3:42, Raiko in 3:44.4.

Announcements of the times drew handclapping and cheers. Several times during the weekend meet, however, spectators surprised the Americans by whistling shrilly—the Russian equivalent of booing. For the most part, though, the crowd was pleased, especially with the final scores. In past meets, the United States men had come out ahead, and to offset these scores the Soviet Union had combined their men's and women's team totals in order to produce a winning score. But this time the Soviet men out-pointed the United States men, 118 to 112, and the combined men's and women's scores gave the hosts a big victory.

By the time he left the Soviet Union, Jim was enjoying both the competition and the comradeship very much. From Kiev, the American team traveled to Poland and West Germany. Ryun was seeing the world—and loving it. Many months afterward someone would ask, "Jim, doesn't it ever bother you that you're missing so many of the pleasures that an average American teen-ager enjoys?"

Jim shook his head. "No," he replied wisely. "After all, how many kids my age go to Kiev?"

In Warsaw, Poland, the Americans won their meet against the Polish national team. Jim's time for the 1,500-meters was only 3:49.9, but it was fast enough to win.

By then, his suitcases were bulging with souvenirs

and gifts. For Edmiston, he had picked out a big metal beer mug decorated with elaborate designs. He bought a cuckoo clock in West Germany. It would look fine on the Ryuns' living room wall, he decided. The portion of the trip that Jim enjoyed most was a scenic bus trip across the Alps from Augsburg, Germany, to Innsbruck, Austria.

In Augsburg, he had stomach trouble and was advised not to run if he felt ill. But Jim felt that he had come all the way to Europe to run, and if he didn't run now he would be defeating his purpose. So he ran—and won the 1,500 in 3:41.6.

That was Jim's last race in Europe. A few days later, he found himself enjoying the mountain air again, but it was the cool, fresh air of the Rocky Mountains in Colorado. Jim, Jeanette, and their mother and father drove to Colorado Springs for a visit with Jim's grandparents, then went west over the Continental Divide. It was Jim's first real vacation in a long time.

"It's real great sleeping late in the morning," Jim told his family at the start of the motor trip. "I don't think I'm going to run another step until I get to KU."

He meant it when he said it. But it wasn't long before his old habits made him restless. One sunny morning late in August, Jim started trotting up a mountain road, took a deep breath and fell rapidly into stride. Soon he was running fast—and panting hard. Jim thought, "Boy, it sure didn't take me long to get out of shape." That wasn't the reason for his

Ryun breasts the tape to win the 1,500-meter race in Augsburg, West Germany.

shortness of breath, however, as he realized almost immediately. He was running at an elevation far above sea level, where the air is "thin," meaning it contains less oxygen. After ten minutes, he had to stop running. His body simply wasn't conditioned to the high altitude.

On a postcard to Timmons, Jim scribbled that he would see the coach in a few days and that he had gone for a short run "for the heck of it." The note concluded: "I gave up, because of lack of air. You know, there sure isn't much at 9,000 feet."

Timmons was looking forward to coaching Jim again, but when he read the message on the card, his thoughts leaped far ahead to the 1968 Olympics. They would be held in Mexico City, which is on a plateau, 7,400 feet above sea level. There wouldn't be much air at that altitude, either. Timmons realized that, if Jim was going to run in the Olympics, he would have to train himself to function on less oxygen than he was accustomed to. And Timmons intended to make sure that Jim would be ready when the time came.

But to Ryun, the 1968 Olympic Games in Mexico represented a challenge in the distant future. Of more immediate importance was his new role as freshman Jim Ryun of the University of Kansas.

10

Rock, Chalk, Jayhawk

Jim Ryun was one of nearly 2,000 boys who entered the University of Kansas in the autumn of 1965. Much to Jim's discomfort, he happened to be the one recognized by almost everyone. The 172-mile trip from the flatlands of Wichita to the rolling hills of Lawrence transformed the high-school senior into a lowly college freshman, but it didn't reduce his status as one of the world's best milers. His first week on the KU campus taught him swiftly that wherever he walked, from the Kansas Union building high atop twisting Jayhawk Boulevard to the Allen Fieldhouse far below, his fellow students knew him—and stood in awe of his achievements.

Some greeted him cheerily: "Hey Ryun . . . Hi there, Jim." Some said nothing to him, but jabbed their companions as he passed. "That's Jim Ryun, the miler," they would whisper. Others just gaped. Jim found it polite and sensible to speak when spoken to. Otherwise he ignored the stares.

Among Jim's classmates was Gene McClain, his old high-school rival from Salina. Jim also discovered his former opponent from Kansas City Wyandotte, Tom Yergovich, who was a sophomore living in the same dormitory, seven-story Olin Templin Hall. But his old rival from Wichita North was missing. Charlie Harper had turned down a scholarship offer from KU and had gone instead to Kansas State.

Jim did not plan to join a fraternity. But that didn't stop the fraternities from trying to sell themselves to Jim. Several houses sent him letters pointing out how many of their members were track lettermen, or that their locations, close to the stadium or field house, were ideally suited to Jim.

Even without fraternity life, Jim's first semester turned out to be busier than he originally intended. Rich Clarkson, the crack sports photographer of the Topeka newspaper, pointed out to Jim that Topeka was less than a half-hour away from Lawrence by way of the Kansas Turnpike. Would Jim like a part-time job taking news pictures of the KU football games? Jim accepted the job eagerly.

At the opening game, he was entrusted with a long-distance, telephoto-lens camera used for taking shots from the end zone. He snapped three rolls of film that included a sequence of the most important

As a part-time photographer for the Topeka Capital-Journal, *Jim took pictures at KU sports events.*

play of the game. The sequence and an additional picture were used in the Sunday sports section. From then on, Jim was on the *Capital-Journal* payroll. Talking to the photo chief about a starting salary for photography and lab work, Jim mentioned one dollar an hour. Then he wondered if he had been brash. "Is that too much?" he asked. The newspaper paid him $1.75. And the following summer, the paper gave him a full-time job, at $2.00 an hour.

Said Rich Clarkson: "Jim learned the basics faster than anybody I ever saw. The amazing rate at which he absorbs instruction indicates he has great potential as a photographer."

As the two worked together on sports assignments, Clarkson's quiet, wry humor and willingness to help appealed to the boy. So did his matter-of-fact honesty about athletes, athletics and life in general. Jim had a number of casual friendships with fellow athletes at KU, but his demanding schedule prevented him from spending much time with any of them. It wasn't long before the 33-year-old Clarkson became his closest friend.

Jim got up each morning at 5:15, ran down "Daisy Hill" from Templin Hall for a long morning workout in the quiet streets of Lawrence, then returned to

Ryun not only had a heavy schedule of classes and workouts, but he was so bothered by phone calls and visitors that he would often slip off to an unused classroom to study quietly.

Templin for breakfast before reporting to his first class. After a long practice in the afternoon, he passed down the Templin "chow line" with his dinner tray in hand, then went back to his room and sat down promptly at his study desk.

"Ryun, you're too much," he was told by teammate Mike Petterson, who had accompanied him to KU from Wichita East. "You're the only guy in the dorm who doesn't waste time messing around after dinner. Every night you hit the books from seven to ten. What are you trying to do, get good grades or something?"

Jim was, indeed, trying to accomplish a lot. On Sunday, traditionally the college boy's morning to sleep late, he would get up early and put in 20 miles of roadwork, and then attend services at the Church of Christ. Often he would drive to Kansas City for an afternoon pro-football assignment at the Kansas City Chiefs' game, then go to church again that night.

Petterson and the others soon learned, however, that quiet Jim Ryun was no dull grind. Jim often took part in pranks at mealtimes. "Hey, who crammed this orange in my glass?" an indignant buddy would ask. Meanwhile Jim, straining to keep a straight face, would gaze innocently at his own dessert.

The first time a water fight broke out in the dorm, Ryun turned up in the middle of it. Trousers rolled up to his knees, he sloshed around in his bare feet, dodging water-filled balloons. His aim with a waste-basket full of water was unerring. Jim also par-

Ryun was no longer a skinny, shy boy, but a broad-shouldered, poised and confident young man.

ticipated in the successful effort to fling Mike Petterson, clothes and all, into Potter Lake. Shortly afterward, Jim himself splashed ashore, soaking wet and smiling broadly.

As Jim's freshman year wore on, it became clear to Ryun's friends that the once skinny, awkward and shy Jim Ryun was growing into a broad-shouldered, strong and poised young man. As his strength increased, he outgrew his head-wagging running style. As he took on poise, he began to go out on weekend dates with a pretty girl who was a Lawrence high-school senior.

The combination of college, Clarkson's friendship, Jim's job and all his traveling were helping him to develop a pleasing, well-balanced personality. Even his small, confined handwriting began to exhibit bigger swirls and loops—a sign of his growing assurance. Once, while still in high school, Jim had listed his hobby on a KU questionnaire as "running." Of course, running was something he now excelled in,

Jim talks with some admirers before services at the Church of Christ in Lawrence.

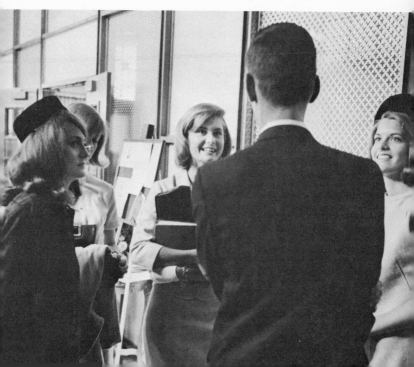

but he confided to Clarkson, "I realize there's something besides track. When I look at Peter Snell taking his wife along and enjoying the world tour, I think that's how I'd like to finish my career. After all, you can't run all your life."

This was an admission that he wouldn't have made to Timmons. Not yet, anyway. Still, Jim remained a dedicated runner. At home in Wichita on Christmas Day, the only reason he passed up his morning workout was that he had a sore throat. But in the afternoon he ran "eighteen holes of golf," a workout devised by Timmons to take some of the drudgery out of training. Jim would start running on the first tee of the golf course, sprint all the way to the first hole, jog to the second tee, then sprint to the hole and continue that way until he completed the entire course.

Before the Sugar Bowl meet in New Orleans a few days later, Jim and varsity runner John Lawson took their 7:00 A.M. workout along the streets of the picturesque French Quarter. Later Jim won his race by 40 yards and broke the meet record for 1,500 meters. He was timed in 3:42.7 and voted top athlete of the meet. Photographers, including Clarkson, were taking pictures of Ryun on the victory stand alongside two other winners. Jim surprised the group by telling Clarkson, "Hey, don't shoot from down there with that wide-angle lens. You'll distort our legs."

When his schedule of invitational indoor meets permitted, Ryun reported to Allen Fieldhouse with his camera. He perched on the bright-red apron of

Ryun and varsity runner John Lawson take their early morning work-out along the streets of the French Quarter before the Sugar Bowl meet in New Orleans.

the KU basketball court. While the cheerleaders led fellow students in bellowing "Rock . . . Chalk . . . Jaaaaayhawk!" Jim Ryun clicked off fast-action photos for the *Capital-Journal*.

While Jim was developing other interests besides running, he also discovered a few troublesome things about track. Reporters hounded him constantly for interviews. Promoters from all over the United States wanted him to run in invitational meets, and every time he ran the crowds insisted on record performances from him.

"There's no way you can satisfy everybody, Jim," advised Timmons. "People want miracles every time you run."

There were other pressures, too. All sorts of problems popped up during Jim's trip to New York City for the New York Athletic Club Games. In order to satisfy all the requests for prerace interviews, Timmons and the meet director set up a short press conference. A writer from *The New York Times* demanded an exclusive interview. At the urging of the meet director, Jim spent five minutes in private with the writer, who then complained loudly that it was impossible to get all the information he needed in such a short time.

The badgering reporters were dissatisfied with Jim's press conferences, too. Jim didn't feel he had to explain his running philosophy—"I don't mind discussing past races, but I'd just as soon not talk about future ones." Many sports writers accused him of avoiding their questions. One nationally syndicated columnist branded him aloof and uppity.

Finally, the famous Baxter Mile—the feature event of the New York Athletic Club meet—was booed by a Madison Square Garden crowd of 15,137, most of whom were eager to see a sub-four-minute mile.

Notre Dame's Eddie Dean set a furiously fast pace, but Ryun and Grelle refused to take the bait. They stayed back and warily watched each other. In the last two laps of the eleven-lap race, Ryun opened up and edged his old rival in 4:02.2. The announcement of Jim's time brought a cascade of boos.

"That was a good tactical race," Jim protested to Timmons. "Couldn't the crowd appreciate that?" Clearly, the crowd couldn't.

Jim was given a television set as his reward for

In the Baxter Mile in New York City, Ryun edged his old rival Grelle (at right) in 4:2.2.

winning the Baxter Mile. Timmons, worried about the boy's amateur status, wrote to the National Collegiate Athletic Association asking permission for Jim to accept the TV set and a typewriter he had received for winning a race in the San Francisco Cow Palace. The NCAA's answer was a swift, sure no. Its ruling: "The only acceptable competitive awards for [amateur] athletes should be medals, trophies, plaques and watches, none of which may exceed the cost figure of $50." The television set and typewriter were packed up and shipped back.

Was Timmons being too cautious in asking the NCAA for a ruling? Jim knew that he wasn't. Both knew the story of Wes Santee, a former KU star. Santee had been accustomed to running the mile in less than 4:10, and on three occasions (before Roger Bannister's record mile) he had come within one second of breaking the four-minute barrier. But in 1955, for a violation of AAU rules prohibiting an athlete from accepting money for participating in sports events, he had lost his amateur standing and had been completely barred from track. To Ryun and the KU coaching staff, the fate of Santee served as a reminder of the perils of offending the AAU.

Later, Jim was to learn that it is possible to offend the AAU in other ways. He didn't want to offend anyone—neither the organization that ruled his sport, nor the spectators who paid the price of admission to enjoy it. But in the weeks just ahead, through no fault of his own, he would displease both groups.

11

Jeers of the Crowd

To satisfy the fans at the Texas Relays, Jim Ryun had to break 4:00 in the mile. It was as simple as that. Nobody had ever run faster than 4:00 in the State of Texas. Premeet publicity for the first big outdoor event of 1966 drew heavily on that theme. The press and promoters of the meet all but promised a sub-four-minute mile by Ryun. Indeed, Jim eagerly hoped to produce one. But Coach Bob Timmons, fully aware of the conflict between Ryun's training schedule and the record hunger of the fans, reminded a Kansas sports writer, "If Jim wants good clockings early in the season, he has to let up in training. We don't want any letups yet. We want him to come to his peak later on. At this point, he's got to keep working hard."

By the time he had run one lap in the Texas Relays

mile, Ryun knew he would set no record that day. A gusty wind was blowing across the track and his legs felt heavy from all the exertion in practice. Impatiently, the crowd of 15,000 hooted as the lap times were announced—:60 . . . 2:06 . . . 3:09. Ignoring the booing, Ryun ran at the speed he thought best-suited to win the race. He timed his last-lap sprint nicely, raced ahead and won by six yards over John Camien, a former Emporia State, Kansas, runner. When the winning time of 4:03.9 was announced, the fans felt cheated. They had no applause for the winner, and a few even booed. The next day several Texas newspapers carried stories cruelly charging that Ryun had deliberately dawdled, sparing himself the effort of a record attempt.

"That's unfair to Jim," stormed Timmons. "All that publicity wasn't his fault. He ran the best race he could."

The knowledge that he had done his best comforted Ryun. He had discovered long ago that there was no way of satisfying everybody. But the fact that a few fans had booed stung his pride. For a long time afterward, he could not forget his experience at the Texas Relays.

The following weekend, in the Southwestern Relays at Lafayette, Louisiana, Jim switched to the two-mile. Foot blisters bothered him, but he won the race in 8:47.4. The week after that, in the Emporia State Relays, he ran the final leg of the four-mile relay for the Kansas Frosh. He came in with a 3:58 mile

During his freshman year, Ryun helped to officiate at varsity track meets. Here he calls out lap times to teammate John Lawson at an indoor meet in Allen Fieldhouse.

that enabled the Jayhawks to set a national record of 16:53.9. Right after that, Jim ran three-quarters of a mile for the winning distance medley team. Then he completed his three-part triumph that day by legging a 47.6 quarter-mile as anchor man in the Kansas freshmen's mile-relay victory. It was hard work, indeed, but it showed Timmons that Jim's training was progressing as he had hoped.

Just before the 41st annual KU Relays, in late April, Timmons told him to ease up in practice in order to run a fast race in the Glenn Cunningham Mile. On Thursday, he proved he was ready for an all-out assault in Saturday's Cunningham Mile by running a 3:59 mile on the anchor leg of a distance medley relay. The Kansas frosh set a United States record for the event.

A steady rain fell Friday. As they sat down to dinner in the Templin Hall cafeteria, Ryun and Tom Yergovich wondered if they'd be able to run at all the next day.

"Timmie says, if he has to, he'll keep the maintenance crew out there all night drying out the track," said Jim.

"If we run," Yergovich told him, "remember what I said to you a couple of weeks ago."

"What was that, Tom?"

"With this sore foot of mine, I'm not going to score any points in the mile, anyway. I'm just the guy to set a fast pace for you. Then you take it on your own and knock that meet record from here to Wichita."

Jim remembered that Timmons had approved of Yergovich's unselfish idea the week before. But at the same time the coach had warned that such pacesetting tactics are illegal unless the so-called "rabbit" completes the race. However fast Ryun might run, there would be no record if Yergovich was unable to finish.

"I'll finish," vowed Tom. "Even if it takes me six minutes."

Late Friday night, the rain stopped. When the gray dawn arrived, Timmons and his ground crew were already at work on the track. The cinder strip felt firm when Ryun tested it a half-hour before his race. He and rival John Camien shook hands at the starting line. Then Tom Yergovich grasped Ryun's hand.

"Runners, go to your marks . . . get set . . ." Crack! Sophomore Yergovich tore into the lead and sprinted around the first turn. Freshman Ryun followed him by about two strides. Camien followed Ryun, another yard back. They stayed in that

Ryun passes "rabbit" Tom Yergovich during the 1966 Glenn Cunningham Mile.

order for almost two laps. Rounding the turn coming into the homestretch, Yergovich felt the painful strain on his tightening muscles. It became unbearable.

"Go get it, Jim," he panted. Then he fell back abruptly.

Ryun passed the half-mile mark in 1:58.7 and the three-quarter pole in 3:00.7. Then he drew away from Camien and dashed around the track to the sound of mounting applause. He was alone, running against the clock. Although there was no one to force him to his best now, he ran as he had never run before. He snapped the tape in 3:55.8, just a half-second off his American record. He had also run the fastest mile in the world for 1966.

Now, Coach Timmons knew, Jim Ryun was on schedule for a world-record mile. Even more important, Jim Ryun was at last sure he could do it, too.

As he trotted across the infield to pick up his sweat suit, Jim threw back his head and inhaled happily. He still felt strong—not nearly as tired as he'd been after beating Snell at San Diego the previous June.

"I feel good, not heavy," he told the reporters as they clustered around. "Let's just say that I'm quite pleased." To Clarkson, he later added, "I feel there'll be some good times this spring."

Few of the reports detected that Jim Ryun, in his modest way, was alerting them to the possibility of a world record ahead.

Then Jim thanked Tom Yergovich, who had struggled painfully home in 4:27. "I thought we had a

Ryun looks exhausted but pleased after winning the Cunningham Mile.

good chance when you hit that half-mile so fast," Jim told him.

"Man, you hit the half, not me," answered Tom. "Right then I felt like I had run a thousand miles and *you* still had the worst half to go. You deserve all the credit for this one."

Jim's response was to give his first-place prize, an engraved watch, to Yergovich.

Ryun's 3:55.8 mile broke Wes Santee's twelve-year-old meet record by more than seven seconds. Three hours later, he finished off his outstanding KU

Relays performance with a 47-second quarter-mile. Although he started off 15 yards behind his anchor-leg opponent, he won the mile relay for Kansas.

To Timmons and Clarkson, probably the two persons who knew him best, Jim's new confidence after the KU Relays was apparent. Going into his next race —the two-mile in the Los Angeles Coliseum Relays— Jim felt better than he could ever remember. He didn't have his normal jitters. And for a change, he wasn't subjected to publicity pressure. The promoters were boasting about "the greatest two-mile field of all time," but they weren't really talking about Ryun. He had run only seven two-mile races in competition, and his best time was 14 seconds slower than the next best runner in the field.

The Los Angeles promoters, in fact, tried to steer Ryun into the one-mile. But Timmons said no. Track experts thought there was a good possibility that a two-mile record would be set in the Coliseum, but their bets were on Jim Grelle, Tracy Smith and the long-distance ace from Kenya, Kipchoge Keino. Keino had caught the fancy of the crowds everywhere in the United States. He always wore an orange baseball cap. When the time came for the African to start his sprint, he flipped off the cap—unless he thought he might lose. On those rare occasions, he left the broad-peaked cap on his head.

With a full 500 yards to go in the Los Angeles race, Keino brought most of the 17,253 Coliseum fans to their feet by whipping off the orange cap and starting to sprint. "If he can keep up that pace, he can have it," thought Ryun, who had been content to run last most of the way. But Jim increased his own speed and startled the crowd. Keino soon found himself overextended. Instead of frightening off all his rivals with an early surge, he had brought Ryun to life. Grelle also had a great deal of strength left. Ryun and Grelle both swept wide on the final turn. Although he was well ahead of Keino, Jim barely managed to hold off Grelle. At the finish Jim was slightly ahead, and both were clocked in 8:25.2. It was an American record, 22 seconds faster than Ryun had ever run the

Keino, Grelle and Ryun round a turn during the two-mile race in the Los Angeles Coliseum Relays.

two-mile distance before, and only 2.6 seconds off the world mark held by Michel Jazy of France.

"I ran out of my gourd," laughed Jim in delight as he and Clarkson discussed the race. It was true that Jim's own strength had surprised him, but mainly because the two-mile distance was still unfamiliar. In the mile, he had a good idea of what he could do.

All over the world, wherever track was a major sport, fans talked about the incredible Kansas teenager. What would he do next? In the Los Angeles *Herald-Examiner*, track expert Harley Tinkham wrote, "There are no limits on Jim Ryun. Before he's through he may own every world record from 800 meters to 5,000 meters."

Jim's next appearance at Los Angeles was in the Compton Relays, and he made his big effort in the mile. Unfortunately, the official who was stationed at the finish line to call out lap times waited until the runners had already passed before shouting out their clockings. Jim couldn't hear him at all. But the crowd heard his time and roared encouragement. With 600 yards to go, Ryun darted away from Grelle and won by 20 yards in 3:53.7, only a tenth of a second over Frenchman Jazy's world mark.

"Ryun would have broken the record if the speakers were set up so we could hear the lap times," insisted Grelle. "And he would have broken it, anyway, if the mile had been run an hour earlier. The track was so chewed up by the time we ran that it must have cost him more than a full second."

Secretly, Jim was disappointed over his clocking at Compton. He recovered so fast after the race that he knew Grelle was right about the lap times. He could have run faster. And he reasoned that the Compton meet offered his last good chance of the season to clip Jazy's record. In the upcoming United States Track and Field Federation meet at Terre Haute, Indiana, he would run the half-mile and probably several relays. In the AAU meet in New York, he would have to concentrate on the opposition in the mile event rather than the clock, because the meet was to determine the United States team for the upcoming competitions with the Russians and Poles. But a mile record in the two international meets was out of the question, because Ryun's event would be run at the international distance, that is, 1,500 meters, rather than the slightly longer mile.

Track politics marred the trip to Terre Haute, however. The AAU, battling to keep control of the sport out of the hands of the National Collegiate Athletic Association, labeled the NCAA-supported Federation meet "unsanctioned." The AAU threatened to bar any athletes who competed there.

Jim didn't want to be drawn into the battle. Timmons, who belonged to the Track and Field Federation, concluded that no organization in the world could be so hungry for power that it would hinder Jim Ryun at this point in his career. So, despite the warning of an AAU official, Timmons decided to allow his boys to compete. Under the banner of the Jayhawk Track Club, they hustled off to Indiana.

They left just in time to avoid a tornado that spun crazily across Kansas. In their dormitory room on the Indiana State campus, Jim and John Lawson listened to radio network commentator Paul Harvey describe the damage in Topeka. They wouldn't learn until later that the house of photographer Rich Clarkson had been one of those destroyed by the terrible twister. Luckily, Clarkson was not hurt.

Just over an hour before the final race at Terre Haute, Ryun had to run a qualifying race in the 880. Originally, a qualifying heat had been scheduled in the mile, too. But meet officials canceled it in order to lure Ryun into the mile final on the following afternoon. They argued that Ryun's very presence meant that he had to run the mile. If he didn't, the meet would be ruined, they contended. Timmons consented, but reminded Jim that his preparations had been mainly for the 880.

Jim wasn't disturbed by the unusual track, a dark asphalt composition strip. His time of 1:50 in the half-mile trial convinced him that his goal of 1:46 was possible. But he wondered if it would be fast enough to win the race.

In the final, Jim ran his first lap in 53.1 seconds. He was third as the runners entered their final lap, still third as they rounded the turn into the backstretch. Jim didn't know how much final effort to expect from his rivals, but he felt good enough to start his own kick with 300 yards left. The fans shouted and stomped their feet on the wooden bleachers as Ryun flashed ahead. With 200 yards to go, he was tearing along at top speed, 10 yards in the lead. With 100 yards to go, he looked back and saw, to his astonishment, that the closest runner was at least 20 yards behind. He plunged forward and broke the tape. Wide-eyed timers in the shadowy finish line area clicked their stopwatches and gathered in a chattering huddle.

"It's a world record," came the shout. Ryun had run his second lap in a stirring 51.8 seconds and his final furlong in an incredible 25.5., covering the unfamiliar half-mile distance in 1:44.9. He had smashed Peter Snell's mark by two-tenths of a second.

The next day, Jim ran a routine 4.02.8 mile and added a 47.8 quarter-mile in a relay. It was of little national concern that a group called the Jayhawk Track Club had won the team title in a breeze. What mattered was that, in a span of five weeks, a 19-year-old youth from Wichita had broken American records in the one-mile and two-mile, as well as a world record in the half-mile. What next, indeed, for Jim Ryun?

Track fans around New York City were particularly interested in Jim's next achievement because nobody had run even a 4:00 outdoor mile in their area. The results of the National AAU meet, at Randall's Island in New York City, would determine the United States team that was to face Poland (at Berkeley, California) and the Soviet Union (at Los Angeles)

In the AAU meet at Randall's Island, Grelle, Burleson and the other

in July. The AAU race would also be, as far as Jim Ryun knew, his last scheduled one-mile competition of the track season.

A crowd of about 16,500 came to Triboro Stadium on the day of the mile, hoping to see Ryun cut loose.

runners all but conceded the race to Ryun. Here Ryun hits the tape.

There were groans in the concrete stands as the entire field, including Ryun, Grelle and Burleson, stayed closely knotted through a slow first lap. One of the timers shook his head disconsolately.

The pace stayed slow. All of the athletes obviously

agreed with Burleson: "The first thing in this meet is that gold medal. It's more important to be the fastest American than to have the fastest time."

After three laps, Ryun led Grelle by one yard and Burleson by four yards, but his time was only 3:06.1 and the crowd booed loudly. Confident that his sprint could match anyone's, Ryun waited until 200 yards remained before making his move. Then he pulled easily away from the pack and bolted to the finish line fast enough to record a victory in 3:58.6.

Naturally, Ryun's win was no upset. But close followers of the sport jerked to attention when they realized that Ryun had run the last lap in 52.6— more than three seconds faster than Michel Jazy had run the last lap of his world-record mile at Rennes, France, in 1965. A few track enthusiasts also noticed something else about the finish of the AAU mile—the strategy of veterans Burleson and Grelle. Both runners had paid little attention to Ryun, and each had concentrated mainly on beating the other for the second 1,500-meter spot on the United States team. They had all but conceded the race to Ryun. In other words, they were admitting that the 19-year-old runner had proved himself the master miler in America.

That would have been the extent of Jim's triumph during the 1966 outdoor season, if it hadn't been for international politics. Six days before the first scheduled international meet, Moscow announced that the Russian team had voted not to run against the United

States. Few track people doubted that the Soviet government, and not the track team, had arranged the pull-out as a protest against the stepped-up role of the United States in the war in Vietnam. Poland's team promptly followed with its own refusal to compete at Berkeley.

Hurriedly, the meets were renamed. The Berkeley meet became the All-American Invitational and the Los Angeles meet became the International Games. And more important, the 1,500-meter event at Berkeley was changed to a one-mile run.

"I'm disappointed," said Jim Ryun. "I worked all year long for this one," referring to the 1,500-meter. But at least he had another crack at Jazy's mile record. At Lawrence, he continued his workouts in the stifling July heat. In the middle of the week, in his role as a *Capital-Journal* photographer, he lugged his camera to St. Louis to cover the major league All-Star baseball game, which was played in 105-degree heat.

On Friday night he reported to United States team coach Stan Wright in Berkeley, California. On Sunday morning, Wright met Ryun in the elevator of their University of California dormitory. "Hey, Coach, I've been thinking," Ryun hailed him. "I'd like to run the 880 in Los Angeles."

Wright, who didn't know Ryun well, was dismayed. "Let's talk about it later," he advised gently. "Your mind ought to be on today's mile."

"I'm thinking about today's mile," replied Jim confidently. "But I also want to run the 880 next week."

Wright couldn't help wondering about Jim's mental readiness for the mile that day. Several hours later, his doubts were put to rest—and so was the best-known mark in the annals of track and field. At 19, Jim Ryun had surpassed the achievements of all the milers who had ever lived. He had run the mile in a world-record 3:51.3.

Since the new holder of the mile record was a boy still in his teens, the track experts immediately started asking, "How fast will he eventually run?" Ryun was reluctant to talk about it. Former Kansan Wes Santee agreed with Jim Grelle, who said, "Jim is capable of running 3:50 any time now." But Santee added a pessimistic comment.

"The problem is," he warned, "Jim has already conquered the world as a teen-ager. If he can sustain a burning desire to improve at track, there's no telling how fast he will run. But I'm afraid the desire will cool. From now on, other things may look more important to him. What has he to look forward to?"

It was up to Jim Ryun to supply the answer.

12

Man of the Year

As an Oakland Raider halfback swung toward the sidelines, the photographer tensed. The play was coming in his direction. He cocked his camera. The football crowd in Kansas City Municipal Stadium roared as one of the Kansas City Chiefs hurtled past a blocker and spilled the ball carrier at the photographer's feet. The shutter clicked and the photographer hopped nimbly aside, avoiding the heavily padded players who crashed to the ground together. As the teams lined up for the next down, a husky voice behind Ryun rasped, "Hey, can I have your autograph?"

Impatiently, Ryun replied, "Just a minute, when this play is over."

As the play ended, Ryun turned and was startled when he realized who had asked for his autograph. It

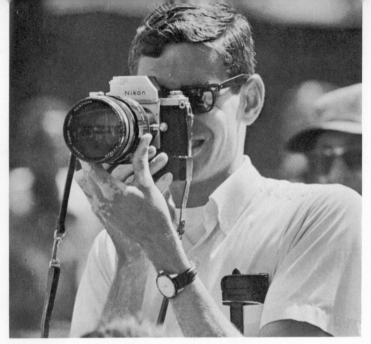

Ryun photographs a KU track meet.

was bewhiskered, 236-pound linebacker E. J. Holub of the Chiefs.

Unfortunately, no spectators were close enough to hear Holub. They would have appreciated the twist of a veteran professional asking a youngster for an autograph. Few of the fans at the Chiefs' home games during the 1966 American Football League season realized that one of the scurrying pack of newspaper photographers was a sports celebrity in his own right. In fact, in the six months that followed Jim's world-record mile at Berkeley, KU athletic publicity director Jay Simon answered the requests of Ryun fans by mailing out more than 300 autographed photographs of Jim.

As a photographer, Ryun was rapidly proving himself. One of his action pictures of Kansas City halfback Mike Garrett appeared in the annual edition of *Best Sports Stories* as one of the finest sports photos of the year. His picture story of a Topeka family washing its dog won third prize in a Kansas-Missouri contest. He also covered the National AAU Women's Cross-Country Meet in St. Louis for *Sports Illustrated*. The only reason his newspaper didn't send him to snap pictures of the National AAU Decathlon Championships in Salina, Kansas, was Rich Clarkson's fear that a track assignment might put Jim's amateur standing in peril.

Early in the fall, Jim sprained his back while jumping over a gully on the KU cross-country course. He missed five weeks of practice. One of Jim's high school buddies from Wichita told a KU teammate, "If Jim had missed that much running when he was younger, he would have bitten his nails off. But now, just look at him. He's taking it right in stride."

Jim's dedication to running hadn't slackened, though. He merely had a number of growing interests outside of track. Almost sadly, Coach Timmons recalled Jim's high school days, when he had no other interests at all. Timmons remembered telling a friend, "I hope Jim never finds out there are girls in East High as well as boys."

Both Timmons and Ryun could feel a change in their old father-and-son relationship. An example of their differences in opinion occurred during a television interview with Ryun that CBS filmed for a show on physical fitness. During the interview, Jim was asked a familiar question: "How fast do you think you can run the mile?" Instead of avoiding an answer, as he had in the past, this time Jim explained patiently, "Considering my rate of progress so far, I think it's logical to assume I'll be able to run the mile under 3:50."

As he spoke, Jim sneaked a quick look at Timmons, who was standing behind the grinding camera. The stunned coach, always wary of predictions, looked as if someone had just slapped him in the face.

In editing the show, CBS snipped out the question and answer entirely. The film editor, not a sports fan, didn't realize that the world champion had put himself on record with a newsworthy prediction. Later, Jim's words were published and many track followers, all over the world, read his mature analysis.

"If I can just word it right," said Jim in response to criticism of his prediction, "I don't see why I shouldn't say what everyone knows. I don't want to sound cocky, but I feel a little stupid every time somebody asks me and I tell him I'm just trying to keep improving. It's obvious that if I improve very much, I'll run a mile under 3:50. I hope that's not egotistic."

Interviews, invitations and phone calls grew more frequent as the school year wore on. Jim's fan mail increased to several dozen letters each week. One letter from overseas arrived bearing the address: "Jim Ryun, Wonder Miler, U. S. A. " Many organizations voted to give Jim their athlete-of-the-year award. However, most of them would not make the award unless he appeared at their banquets in person. But Jim's activities didn't leave him enough time to accept the offers. Timmons wailed, "If Jim accepted even half of these invitations, he wouldn't have time to keep up with his schoolwork, much less keep up with his training."

To Clarkson, Jim confided, "I want to live my own life a little bit. I've got to say 'no' to things. People are trying to use all my free time."

The awards continued. The "Kansas Comet," as one Associated Press writer dubbed Jim, received a huge trophy for being selected Sportsman of the Year by *Sports Illustrated* magazine. The inscription on the trophy read, "Sportsman of the Year 1966, Jim Ryun, for symbolizing in character and performance the ideals of sportsmanship." Twelve years earlier, the magazine's first sportsman award had gone to the runner who broke the four-minute barrier, England's Roger Bannister.

The Swedish newspaper *Aftonbladet*, after polling sports editors in 23 countries, voted Jim Ryun Athlete of the Year. The American Broadcasting Company's television show, "Wide World of Sports," also picked him as Athlete of the Year. Finally, in February, 1967, Jim won the most significant prize of all —the AAU's James E. Sullivan Award for the top amateur athlete in the United States.

Jim and Timmons flew to Chicago for the presentation. When he was given the trophy, Jim heard a beaming official announce, "If James Ronald Ryun is an example of the courage of today's youth, then this country has nothing to worry about." Later, Jim was introduced at the head-table microphone. His memorized talk lasted no more than 20 seconds.

"The year 1966 was a very, very good one for me," he said. "But it would not have been possible without the help and understanding of my family, coaches and teammates. It is a great honor to accept this Sullivan Award and an even greater honor to join the ranks of the former winners of the Award."

The trip to Chicago was combined with a bitter disappointment, however. There, he learned that his world record for the half-mile, set at Terre Haute eight months earlier, still had not received approval from the International Amateur Athletic Federation. The AAU of the United States had submitted Ryun's

Mr. William G. Mason, vice-president of the Quaker Oats Company, presents the Sullivan Award trophy to Jim.

record, unsigned, to the world group, along with a comment that the record was set in an unsanctioned meet. The AAU hinted that it might approve the mark if the Track and Field Federation would apply for sanction.

The Big Eight Conference, to which KU belonged, promptly issued a formal protest. It stated, "This is an unjustified effort by the AAU to use an athlete as a weapon against the U. S. Track and Field Federation. We ask that the AAU be ordered to resubmit the record for international approval on the basis of the record itself and without the prejudicial comment which reportedly accompanied the original."

To make matters worse for Jim, the Federation again maintained that it did not need AAU recognition and refused to ask for sanction for the meet. As a pawn in the power struggle between two rival groups, Jim came out as the loser. The IAAF turned down the record application for Ryun's 1:44.9 half-mile because the application lacked AAU approval. Technically, Peter Snell's old mark of 1:45.1 was still the world record.

Throughout the winter, Jim ran only twice in invitational meets. He was a member of the Kansas varsity now and team obligations came first. Running in fewer meets removed a lot of the pressure that had existed in Jim's freshman year. As a sophomore, he had more leisure time and he began to enjoy himself. In February, 1967, he finally went to his first dance—and had a wonderful time.

Ryun struggles vainly to overtake Villanova's Dave Patrick.

In March, at the NCAA Indoor Championship in Detroit's Cobo Arena, another "first" occurred. This new experience, however, was one Jim didn't enjoy. For more than a year, Villanova junior Dave Patrick had been eagerly looking forward to his first race against Ryun. They met at last in Detroit. Since the KU team needed as many points as it could win, Jim was entered in a number of events. On Friday afternoon, he had to run in a qualifying heat for the half-mile. So did Patrick. But Ryun also had to run a qualifying mile less than two hours before the 880 final that night. Patrick skipped the mile and came into the 880 far more rested. Even more important, he was closer to his physical peak than Ryun, who had been adhering to a training schedule that lead to a peak later in the year—July or August.

The blond Patrick dashed into the lead at the start and pulled away steadily. His time for the first quarter was a speedy 52.4. Ryun didn't think Patrick could keep up the pace. He decided to stay back, waiting for the Villanova runner to stiffen. Suddenly three more runners shot past. By the time Jim got back around them, Patrick was 35 yards ahead. Patrick didn't stiffen, either. Ryun's head swerved from side to side as he forced himself to make up distance, but he couldn't make up enough. Patrick won by 15 yards. His time was 1:48.9, a world indoor record.

It was Ryun's first setback in a major race in almost two years. He had been favored in most of them and finally he found himself in the role of a beaten favorite. It was almost a relief to have his string of victories broken.

"Maybe it's all for the best," he said sadly. "Maybe it will prove to people that I'm human after all, that I can suffer pain, that I can be beaten. Maybe now some of the pressure will be off."

In Jim's estimation, most of the pressure was lifted the following afternoon. In the mile final, he left the rest of the field far behind, won by a full 40 yards and ran the second fastest indoor mile on record, 3:58.6. "That Friday defeat helped to spur me on," he admitted. "I'm glad the indoor season is over now. I've always been afraid of injury indoors and the boards are hard on my feet. I'm looking forward to running outdoors."

In the KU Relays, Jim ran a 3:54.7 mile, the fastest ever run so early in the outdoor track season. It was also Jim Ryun's last mile as a teen-ager. The following weekend, at the Drake Relays in Des Moines, Iowa, he celebrated his 20th birthday. (He was born on April 29, 1947.) By Saturday night, though, he was celebrating more than his birthday. The day before, his 3:59.1 mile in the anchor leg of the four-mile relay had led Kansas to a victory. On Saturday afternoon, his 3:55.6 mile not only had bettered Friday's mark, but it also had enabled the Jayhawks to set a world record in the distance medley relay. Jim's mile times were the fastest in the history of the meet.

Jim's next big race was the Los Angeles Coliseum–Compton Invitational. Although there was little competition to set a fast pace, Jim finished 70 yards ahead of the next runner and ran the world's second-fastest mile—3:53.2.

Wes Santee's fears that other interests might interfere with Jim's track career were obviously groundless. In addition to his determination to better his achievements, Jim was stimulated by the prospect of competing in the 1968 Olympic Games in Mexico City. Only his closest friends were aware of his deep feelings about making up for his early elimination in the 1964 Olympics at Tokyo.

National teams are forbidden by Olympic rules to train for more than a month at high-altitude sites, but there is no rule forbidding an individual to spend as much time as he likes in the mountains. Jim was looking ahead to the competition in Mexico City so earnestly that he accepted an invitation to spend several weeks of June, 1967, training at Adams State College in Alamosa, Colorado, 7,400 feet above sea level.

"At first, running at that altitude was frightening," Ryun admitted afterward. "It was like having something in your throat and chest that kept you from breathing. But then it got easier all the time. When you come down and run at a normal altitude, you can't get over feeling how much air there is."

The National AAU championships in Bakersfield, California, were next on Ryun's schedule. Along with Jim, nine others were entered in the mile, including Jim Grelle, Tom Von Ruden and Martin Liquori, a 17-year-old high-school boy from New Jersey. By the day of the race, Ryun was so impatient for a record that the competition—or rather, the lack of it—couldn't hold him back.

Grelle was no longer able to keep up with Ryun. Neither was Von Ruden. As Ryun raced past the half-mile mark in 1:59, he knew that he would win, but he felt a twinge of disappointment because the pace did not seem fast enough for a record. Opening up his stride in the third lap, he pulled away from the others for his fastest lap of the race so far—58:6. To the crowd of 10,000 in the high, double-decked stadium, it seemed unbelievable that Ryun could pour on even more speed in his final quarter-mile. Faster and faster, he galloped around the track for the last time, finishing 40 yards ahead of Grelle to the sound of wild cheers and applause. His time for the final lap was 53.5 seconds. His total time was an astounding 3:51.1.

Even though he had run without competition to spur him on, he had broken his own world record by two-tenths of a second and had finished a full five seconds ahead of runner-up Grelle. Going almost unnoticed, six other runners, including Martin Liquori, finished in under four minutes.

To track fans it seem obvious that Ryun had responded marvelously to his high-altitude work. However, Jim himself discounted the popular theory that training in oxygen-thin air improved an athlete's endurance at sea level. He felt that the benefits of his work in the mountains were confined strictly to running at high altitudes. Whether Ryun was right or not, track fans everywhere became excited when they learned that he intended to run the 1,500-meters against another high-altitude trainee, Kipchoge Keino. Keino had trained in Nyeri, Kenya, 5,900 feet above sea level.

The two now-familiar rivals met at the Los Angeles Coliseum on July 8, 1967, in a meet between teams of the United States and British Commonwealth. Conditions were far from ideal. There was a light smog, and the temperature was 90 degrees.

Indeed, the possibility of a world record seemed doomed when Keino immediately dropped back into fifth place and Ryun, refusing to set the pace, settled into sixth. Suddenly, at the start of the second lap,

Ryun training in the San Luis Valley, near Alamosa, Colorado.

Keino blazed past everyone else and took the lead. Ryun, racing with amazing smoothness, quickly made up the distance and followed along in second place. They ran that way for two brisk laps.

Then Ryun sped up and drove past Keino, gradually picking up more speed as he pulled ahead. He began his sprint with 300 yards to go. Both the crowd and Keino were astounded at the ease with which Ryun opened the gap and drove relentlessly to the tape. He finished a full 30 yards ahead of the struggling Kenyan.

Few were astonished, however, when it was announced that Ryun had broken the world record set by Herb Elliott in the 1,500-meter race of the Rome

Olympics seven years earlier. Ryun's time was 3:33.1, fully 2.5 seconds faster than the old record.

About an hour later, sipping on a soft drink and smiling, Jim said candidly, "I still don't feel my limit has been reached. I can go faster."

How much faster—and at how many different distances—the track world has yet to learn. Looking ahead to the Mexico City Olympics, Ryun remembered Peter Snell's gold medal performances in the 800- and 1,500-meter races in Tokyo, but he doubted that he would make the same effort. Jim intended to concentrate on the 1,500.

Could he lower the 1,500-meter mark again, despite the difficulties of top-notch competition at such a high elevation? Some experts have insisted that a record at that distance is impossible in Mexico City.

Impossible? Once it was thought that no human being could ever run a mile in less than four minutes. And of course it was beyond imagination that a mere stripling of a high-school boy might accomplish such a feat someday.

Yet Jim Ryun's deeds seem to deny the finality of the word "impossible." And it is a fact that all of his amazing achievements have been reached at an age long before most athletes arrive at their prime. Where Jim Ryun of Wichita, Kansas, is concerned, only one thing seems truly impossible—forecasting the dazzling future that his talent and will power are likely to provide.

Index

Page numbers in italics refer to photographs

About the Author

Formerly a sports writer with the New York *Herald Tribune*, John Lake is now the sports editor at *Newsweek* magazine. He conceived the idea for the present book after writing a *Newsweek* cover story about Jim Ryun. Through interviews with Ryun, his family, friends and coaches, he has been able to put together an exciting biography of the most outstanding competitor in track today.